The
EVERYTHING
COLLEGE
MAJOR
TEST BOOK

Dear Reader,

"What can I do with a major in _____?" There is no simple answer to this question, but now there are simple steps you can take to find the answers for yourself. Are you a high school student trying to connect possible majors to college applications? Are you a college student facing a deadline to declare your major? Are you graduating soon and feeling pressure from your parents to do something with your major? Whoever you are, this book will help you learn about yourself, possible majors, and relevant careers. Completing the exercises and activities in *The Everything® College Major Test Book* will help you research and assess various majors, link them to your values, skills, and academic interests, and help you choose the major that's right for you.

The noun "major" is defined as a field of study chosen as an academic specialty. As an adjective, "major" describes something of great importance. While it's important to choose a major, don't exaggerate its significance—that will only make you anxious. But don't procrastinate, either. This book will help you through the process and ease your fears. Relax and read on!

The EVERYTHING® Series

Editorial

Publishing Director	Gary M. Krebs
Director of Product Development	Paula Munier
Associate Managing Editor	Laura M. Daly
Associate Copy Chief	Brett Palana-Shanahan
Acquisitions Editors	Gina Chaimanis
	Lisa Laing
Development Editor	Jessica LaPointe
Associate Production Editor	Casey Ebert

Production

Director of Manufacturing	Susan Beale
Associate Director of Production	Michelle Roy Kelly
Cover Design	Paul Beatrice
	Matt LeBlanc
	Erick DaCosta
Design and Layout	Colleen Cunningham
	Sorae Lee
	Jennifer Oliveira
Series Cover Artist	Barry Littmann

Visit the entire Everything® Series at *www.everything.com*

THE
EVERYTHING®
COLLEGE MAJOR
TEST BOOK

10 tests to help you choose the major that is right for you

Burton Jay Nadler

Author of *The Everything® Resume Book*

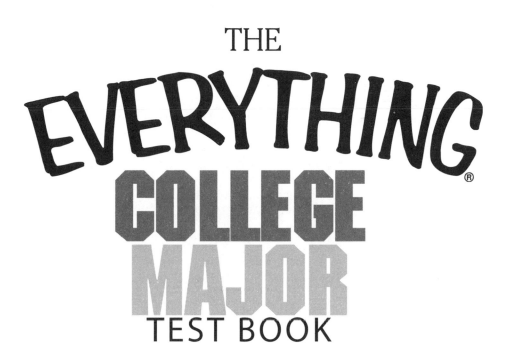

Adams Media
Avon, Massachusetts

Dedication
To the thousands who over the decades have asked, "What can I do with a major in _____?"
You found answers and, ultimately, success. Keep testing yourselves.
To Jordan and Justin: You continue on your paths to majors, careers,
and happiness and make me a very proud poppa.

———————————————————————————

An Everything® Series Book.
Everything® and everything.com® are registered trademarks of F+W Publications, Inc.

Published by Adams Media, an F+W Publications Company
57 Littlefield Street, Avon, MA 02322 U.S.A.
www.adamsmedia.com

ISBN: 1-59337-591-3
Printed in the United States of America.

J   I   H   G   F   E   D   C   B   A

Library of Congress Cataloging-in-Publication Data
is available from publisher.

This publication is designed to provide accurate and authoritative information with regard to the subject matter covered. It is sold with the understanding that the publisher is not engaged in rendering legal, accounting, or other professional advice. If legal advice or other expert assistance is required, the services of a competent professional person should be sought.

—From a *Declaration of Principles* jointly adopted by a Committee of the American Bar Association and a Committee of Publishers and Associations

Many of the designations used by manufacturers and sellers to distinguish their products are claimed as trademarks. Where those designations appear in this book and Adams Media was aware of a trademark claim, the designations have been printed with initial capital letters.

This book is available at quantity discounts for bulk purchases.
For information, please call 1-800-872-5627.

Contents

Top Ten Majors
in the United States

1. Business (21 percent of degrees conferred)

2. Education (9 percent of degrees conferred)

3. Health professions and related sciences

   (6 percent of degrees conferred)

4. Psychology (6 percent of degrees conferred)

5. Engineering (5 percent of degrees conferred)

6. Visual and performing arts (5 percent of degrees conferred)

7. Computer and information sciences (4 percent of degrees conferred)

8. Liberal arts and sciences, general studies, and humanities

   (3 percent of degrees conferred)

9. Multi/interdisciplinary studies (2 percent of degrees conferred)

10. Protective services (2 percent of degrees conferred)

Introduction

▶Who are you? Are you a high school student thinking about college? Maybe you are a college freshman freaking out about choosing your courses. You may be a college sophomore anxious about your deadline for declaring a major or a senior trying to identify and act upon your post-baccalaureate options. Perhaps you are a parent who is concerned about your child's major, college costs, and potential career payoffs. Have you asked yourself, "What can I do with a major in _____?" or "How do I choose a major?" Or have your parents asked you about your future plans, with your only response a confused expression?

Seeking answers, you have perused library and bookstore shelves and searched online. The many resources you found have only added to your confusion. You may have come across the various encyclopedic publications that list hundreds of majors and information on the colleges that offer them. A few resources deal with the process of declaring a major and some of the psychological issues that impact that effort. One or two address issues specifically related to liberal arts majors. Some volumes describe possible career options. A few contain some self-assessment exercises that purport to provide you with a general sense of yourself and your aspirations.

The Everything® College Major Test Book is different from all of those. It walks you through a variety of fun self-assessment exercises, guides you as you create some powerful summary profiles, and then helps you synthesize all of the information into a picture of *you*—your skills, traits, values, and academic interests—and points you to a major that's right for you right now. Yes, there are lots of tests, but there are no wrong answers. These are tests you cannot fail.

The Danish philosopher Søren Kierkegaard once wrote, "Life can only be understood backwards; unfortunately, we have to live it forward." In your day-to-day academic life, you don't have the perspective to see the whole picture of your potential. If you truthfully complete the tests, exercises, and research recommended in this book, you will produce a self-assessment of what interests you right now, how those interests can help you select a major, and perhaps how they can also lead to a fulfilling career. As you continue your research, you will be able to clarify your desires, prioritize your options, and eventually declare a major with confidence.

The activities that follow will also connect various majors with related jobs, enabling you to plan even further into the future of your working life. You will gain a new frame of reference for your likes and dislikes in terms of subject areas, work situations, and career options.

Navel-gazing and hoping will not transform your dreams into realities or your feelings into a fruitful academic strategy. The tests in this book are designed to guide you through the process, motivate you, and help you move from one stage of decision-making to the next.

The Everything® College Major Test Book incorporates the best elements of the thousands of resources available. By the time you reach the last chapter, you should be able to declare a realistic, attainable major in a field that interests you. You will even have begun to think about possible graduate-school options or careers related to that major.

But your results depend on the effort you put into it. So read on, follow the advice offered, and complete the activities honestly. This book offers everything you need to successfully declare a major.

Chapter 1
Choosing a Major

To paraphrase Confucius, "Choose a major you love and you will never have to work a day in your life." He was talking about jobs, but the point is the same. People who can match a major to their values, skills, interests, and personality stand a better chance of feeling happy and fulfilled in college. Take the time to find out more about yourself as you start down the path of academic fulfillment. The philosopher also said that a journey of a thousand miles begins with a single step. Take that first step.

Is Picking a Major a Big Deal?

Perhaps you've lived through this scenario: You're a college senior seated with your family at Thanksgiving dinner. Uncle Mortimer smiles at you and says, "Pass the gravy. And by the way, what are you going to do after you graduate, when your ride on the gravy train is over?" Mom, Dad, Aunt Ruth, and your brothers, sisters, and cousins stare at you and await your answer. At a loss for words, you divert their attention by dropping Aunt Ruth's green-bean casserole on the floor.

It's only natural that your post-graduation plans are of interest to your family. After all, they're probably paying for your education and so have some stake in your future success and happiness. You should be able to articulate your intentions with a modicum of focus. What you shouldn't do is interpret Uncle Mortimer's question to mean, "What are you going to do with the rest of your life?" Nor should you whine about the difficulty of completing all your schoolwork, choosing a major, or looking for a job or internship. Uncle Mortimer, and those who ask similar questions, will probably be satisfied with some indication that you have thought about your future and have taken realistic steps to figure it out. And you're in luck—helping you do just that is what this book is for. (Thanking your parents for whatever educational opportunities they've bestowed upon you wouldn't be a bad idea either.)

Picking a major is important, but not in ways that you might think. Putting off your declaration only adds to your anxiety—and you probably have enough of that already. Taking concrete steps to determine your goals and desires, examine your interests, skills, and values, and explore your options will motivate you. You may discover some surprising things about yourself, such as new interests you didn't know you had. The clarity and focus you gain by selecting a major will encourage you to make plans, implement some realistic strategies, and make progress toward your future career path. Learning how to set and meet goals, prioritize, and adapt to changing circumstances will stand you in good stead in the academic world as well as in the "real" world of work.

Your interests and goals will continue to grow and change throughout your life. Picking a major now is not equivalent to signing your life away with a binding contract. You can always change your mind if another field of endeavor captures your attention. Just remember that actions speak louder than words. With the help of this book you no longer need to just talk about declaring a major; you can do it.

"ARM" for Decisions about Your Major

Former U.S. Secretary of State Colin Powell once said, "Be careful what you choose. You may get it." Though you will make other, much more important decisions in your life, deciding on a major will affect the direction of your academic career as well as your satisfaction with your whole educational experience. It's not a life-or-death decision, but your choice of major deserves thoughtful consideration. It isn't enough to vaguely hope for an "interesting" major or dream of someday finding your "true passion." You need to ARM yourself for action.

The acronym "ARM" stands for "assessment, research, making decisions." It's an easy-to-remember way to effectively clarify your goals and eventually focus on a major. Answering questions that assess what you really think and feel, as well as what you're good at, will help you zero in on a major that is tailored to *you*. The tests will also help you articulate your goals clearly, for yourself and anyone who asks. The only way you will discover your options and figure out what is involved in completing the major you think you want is to do some research. Ultimately, all of this work will result in your making a decision and declaring a major.

"A" Is for Assessment

Some students try to pick a major by waiting for inspiration to strike. Others may throw a dart at the college catalog and see what it hits. These methods will result in the choice of a major, but it may not be one you're very good at—or even like. The key to fitting a major to you is assessment. This book contains a variety of true-false tests, questions, and matrices for you to fill out. The tests cover many things, including your values, interests, personality traits, and skills. Such criteria are significant whether you're choosing a major or a job. Do you prefer practical courses, such as accounting, or more theoretical ones, such as philosophy? Are you more concerned with finding a field you love or finding one with the highest earning potential? Do you like to be around people or work with numbers? Do you want to save the planet? Are you a good problem solver, brain-stormer, or negotiator?

Along with the more formal tests administered by testing professionals (such as the Strong Interest Inventory, Myers-Briggs Type Indicator, CISS, and Motivated Skills and Career Values), the informal exercises in this book and the Web sites listed in Appendix B (such as *www.mapping-your-future .org* and *www.petersons.com*) are all useful tools for pinpointing your ideal major. Each chapter helps you analyze your assessment results and focus your research. If you complete the tests honestly, you will end up with a clearer picture of your goals. The tests provide a snapshot of who and where you are now in your academic life, as well as a way to measure whether a major or potential career fits you.

The process of assessment includes all of the following:

- Assessment is done actively, through the completion of tests, activities, exercises, and worksheets. Passive introspection is not enough to clarify and articulate goals or declare a major.
- Assessment is part of a larger process. Taking stock of what you know about yourself and about potential academic and career options will help you understand what you don't know as well as what you do know.
- For some, assessment is best done through formal devices interpreted by professionals; for others, this process is best done through informal tests like those in this book.

The assessment tests included in this book progress from means of gaining initial impressions to tools for determining specific views and personal descriptors. First, using the test in Chapter 2, you will review, identify, and prioritize a lengthy list of majors. Second, the true-false test included in Chapter 4 will reveal your readiness for continued assessment and overall attitudes regarding majors and careers. Next, you will learn of personal characteristics related to values, interests, personality traits, and skills by completing the test in Chapter 5. You may find that the self-knowledge you gain from these initial assessments will give you the insight and confidence you need to take action and choose a major. On the other hand, these informal tests may indicate that you need more information before you can take the next step—or move on from your assessments and actually make a major declaration. That next step involves the "R" in ARM: research.

"R" Is for Research

You already know that research is careful investigation of matter for information or truth. You've no doubt had to do plenty of it for papers and reports throughout your school life. Good research skills can be applied to more than just term papers. You can use them to research majors, the relationship between certain majors and careers, and job functions related to those careers.

Research can involve looking through printed and online resources and talking to knowledgeable people. It provides the critical bridge from confusion to focus, from assessment to declaring a major, and from deciding on a major to ultimate academic and job-search success.

Research Courses

The research associated with deciding on a major includes identifying the requirements for the different majors that interest you; reviewing the course syllabi; comparing and analyzing course content and instructional techniques (for instance, labs, papers, exams, or projects); matching these to your personal learning style and preferences; and recognizing the career implications of any major you may choose. To get you started, review the descriptions at the end of this chapter of some of the most popular majors. The worksheets and matrices in subsequent chapters will help you make sense of all the data you collect, set objectives, and take further action.

Research Careers

As you research the relationships between various majors and careers, you will increase your knowledge of different fields, their functions, and the work settings within those fields. The research will expand your career vocabulary and help you articulate your goals as you become fluent in the language of the world of work.

Research by Asking

In addition to reading, you can find out lots of information by talking to people—either people who majored in fields you're interested in or role models working in careers you're thinking about. Ask them about their academic and practical experiences, and find out about their interests and skills. Internships, co-ops, and externships (basically, the opportunity to shadow a professional performing a job of interest to you) will immerse you in real work environments and help you learn how to complete projects as you observe others. Later chapters identify links between majors, career fields, job functions, and various academic contexts, such as minors and clusters. You will be given ample opportunity to study these and choose the best options for you. Research resources and other tips are provided as you go to help you answer questions and focus on a decision.

"R" Is for Reality Check

Ultimately, "R" really stands for "reality check." The only way to determine the best and most realistic academic options for you is to consider your personal financial, intellectual, emotional, and other circumstances. At the same time, you should try to avoid "analysis paralysis." It is possible to overthink all of this, and it is certainly possible to worry too much about it. Take your courses, declare a major, and focus your career research efforts on two or three options knowing that you can always change your mind later. Should your interests change, you can drop or add courses, add a minor or cluster (as defined on page 10), take one or two courses in other subject areas, or participate in externship and internship opportunities to round out your academic experience. Find a mentor. Take your next step; it's not irrevocable. Move at your own pace along that path toward declaring a major, but keep moving!

Anxiety regarding major decision-making, goal expression, and completion of research can be debilitating. Many people procrastinate at this point because they dread potentially negative consequences, or, more likely, they believe decisions are irreversible. Researching options, learning more about realistic alternatives, and making the connections between majors and careers can help overcome this anxiety and resultant paralysis.

Research involves the following steps:

- Reading books: Look for titles containing the words "careers" or "majors."
- Completing Web-based research: Use key phrases like "majors and careers" in search engines like *www.google.com* or *www.metacrawler.com*.
- Asking questions: Query your role models, mentors, or other people in fields of interest. See Chapter 3 for some sample questions.
- Taking notes: Highlight or otherwise identify the data most useful and relevant to you.

"M" Is for Making Decisions

After beginning to ARM yourself for success by completing the assessments, doing the research, and asking lots of questions, all that remains is to make a decision and declare your major. By the end of this book, you will have a pretty good idea of your interests, your likes and dislikes, how you work, as well as some understanding of the different majors and what is entailed in each. All that remains is to match all of your data to a major.

Majors Are Mutable

Remember, no decision you make now is cast in concrete. You can change it later if you want. You can complete the assessment and research processes again and again as you better understand yourself, your desires, and your goals. You've heard the term "career path," but in reality a career is made up of a series of interconnected paths. Some of them you choose; some of them choose you. Sometimes a relationship between a major and a career is easy to identify, and the path appears straight and clearly marked. Other times the relationship is subtler and takes more effort to identify. These paths can evolve unexpectedly from a minor, an internship, or a two- or three-course cluster. Use your research skills—and your imagination—to seek out the many potential paths available to you and choose the one that's best for you.

Making a decision about a major includes the following steps:

- Identify potential majors and the requirements associated with each.
- Talk to academic advisors, faculty, and students about courses, requirements, and academic issues.
- Review printed and online lists of majors and their required courses and prerequisites.
- Explore and, when appropriate, complete externships and internships.
- Locate academic and career role models and develop relationships with them. These are the people who can become mentors and even advocates in support of your academic career.
- Declare your major and begin to take courses associated with it, confident that you can change your mind, and major, or add courses later.
- Take supplemental post-baccalaureate courses that relate to your preferred career fields.

Vocabulary for Choosing a Major

The essayist and philosopher Francis Bacon once wrote, "If a man will begin with certainties, he shall end in doubts; but if he will be content to begin with doubts, he shall end in certainties." You probably have many doubts concerning your future. Perhaps you have been agonizing for weeks over what to choose for a major. The best time to use this book is during the first semester of your sophomore year of college, but its usefulness extends well beyond that particular time. If you're already in the second semester of your sophomore year, or later, remember this: Better late than never. You have the desire, the need, and now you have the tools at hand to formulate some options and make a decision. Let's clear up those doubts and get started! First, review some vocabulary words that will help you understand what comes later in this book.

In order to major in a particular subject or work in a particular career, you have to be conversant in the vocabulary of that field. As you begin to explore all the potential majors open to you, first study the vocabulary list below. You'll come across these terms as you delve into your self-assessment and research. Familiarizing yourself with the terminology should begin to diminish your anxiety about the process of declaring a major.

Academic Advising

The advising process involves discussions between a student and faculty member, professional in the field, or other students. The goal is to help the student take care of scheduling or curricular issues, such as making sure he or she is completing course requirements or taking the right prerequisites for a given major. Academic advising can transition into career counseling, but the process focuses more on addressing the issues related to school requirements and scheduling.

Assessment

For the purpose of this book, the term "assessment" refers to the evaluation of information about yourself and majors. These assessments take place through formalized, standardized, or self-help tools and tests designed specifically to increase your knowledge of yourself and link that knowledge to majors and careers. There is no one magic test that will give you the answer to the question of which major is best for you. Assessment comes from compiling and analyzing the results of many different tests and lots of research.

Career Counseling

Through the career counseling process, a student connects his or her self-knowledge assessment to real-world career options. A student can undertake the process formally with a professional career counselor; informally with faculty members, family, or friends; or alone, through research and the use of books like this one. Career counseling helps the student learn about opportunities such as internships or part-time jobs. It's a useful way to set short- or long-term goals. Counseling also helps with the job search, from reviewing resumes to practicing interviews. If done effectively, it concludes with the student being able to say, "I know what can I do with a major in _____" and being better able to set realistic, attainable goals.

Cluster

A cluster is a group of two, three, or more thematically linked courses. They may supplement or complement your major and help build and define the academic foundation upon which you build an internship or job search. For example, someone majoring in biology with the intention of going to medical school might take a cluster of courses from the theater, music, and art departments on the uses of art in healing. Just those few focused courses can help broaden your qualifications for various job opportunities. Remember that you can major in anything that fascinates you academically and still pursue other interests through clusters, whether vocationally focused or not.

Concentration

As it relates to college majors, a concentration is a specialization within your major, which you usually complete by taking a cluster of courses related to a particular topic or theme. This can be the focus of your senior thesis or other papers or projects.

Co-op

This is an arrangement, often spanning two semesters or academic quarters, that blends academic study and practical experience. Most co-op students earn credit as well as salaries, so this option is sometimes called "learning while earning" or a "super-internship." Sometimes the co-op is a requirement for a major and must be completed to earn a degree.

Double Major

A double major entails completing the coursework required to major in two subjects, which can result in earning one or two degrees or even a combination degree. Each school has its own rules and requirements for pursuing a double major. This decision increases your college workload considerably, so weigh your options and goals carefully.

Dual Degree

Obtaining a dual degree involves completing the coursework for two distinct degrees, such as a bachelor of arts and a bachelor of science.

Focus

Just as in optics, in choosing a major, focus means a clear image. All of the assessment, research, academic advising, career counseling, and exploration you will do as you work through this book will result in a distinct and clear—focused—picture of the major for you.

Minor

A minor consists of a series of courses—more than a cluster but fewer than those required for a major—that focus on a particular subject, topic, or theme. In addition to minors, some schools offer certificates to recognize the completion of specific groups of thematically linked courses. Many students use minors and certificate programs to take more practical or career-related courses than might be included in their major.

One-Course-at-a-Time Strategy

This is an effective approach to exploring various majors that interest you. Once you hit on something you like, you can continue with more career-related courses in that subject.

Placement

This is the final outcome of your efforts to focus on a major and career. There are a variety of majors, internships, and jobs for everyone. Don't fixate on finding that "perfect" major or job. If you keep your mind on each next step in the process, you will find your place.

Research

Research is defined as careful investigation or study. You no doubt research your options before buying a car, computer, or clothes. Don't you think that finding the subject you will devote yourself to for the next several years deserves at least as much effort? Research is also the step that's most often overlooked on the path to choosing a major and achieving professional success.

Self-Designed Major

Most schools allow students to create their own majors in order to focus on particular intellectual, career, or topical interests or to include multidisciplinary courses in more than one academic department. Creating your own major takes good planning, and perhaps some trial and error, but it's an approach that works well for some students. One caveat: You can't wait until the last minute to create your own major.

Testing

As a student, you are intimately acquainted with tests of all sorts, from essay to multiple-choice to true-false. For the purposes of this book, testing can be achieved through formal devices, such as the Strong Interest Inventory or the Myers-Briggs Type Indicator. But tests can also be informal, such as the true-false ones in this book. These tests are designed to foster your curiosity about the options open to you and to encourage you to explore those options. They will help target your research and ultimately result in a clearer picture of your goals and how to reach them.

Three/Two Program

Sometimes called submatriculation, a three/two program involves beginning a master's degree during what would typically be your senior year in college. Thus, instead of taking four years to earn a bachelor's degree and two more to earn a master's degree, you can earn both degrees in a total of five years.

Vocation, Avocation, Vacation

These words sound alike, and they all relate in some way to your major and career, but they mean quite different things. Your vocation is your job and, as you progress through jobs over the years, your career. In industry parlance it's defined by the three "F"s: field (what category of work you're in), function (what you specifically do), and firm (where you work).

Your avocation is a hobby, special interest, or personal passion that is usually pursued outside of work. Truly lucky people manage to combine their avocation and vocation and get paid for what they love to do.

A vacation, obviously, is what you enjoy when you have time off from school or work. Balancing all three is one key to enjoying a fulfilling academic or work life.

Chapter 2
Majors at First Glance

The old saying, "You never get a second chance to make a good first impression," may be true when it comes to relationships, but it doesn't apply at all when it comes to declaring a major. Rest assured that you will have many opportunities to identify, research, prioritize, and declare your major. Every time you review information about majors, internships, or careers, you learn something new, perhaps even unexpected. Knowing that you can change your mind should boost your confidence about making those initial choices.

College Majors Checklist

This checklist test is designed to assess your first impressions about many different majors and identify some of your current interests. Don't be intimidated by the length of the list, which comprises over thirty general academic fields and over 300 specific majors. Work quickly and check your first reactions. You aren't expected to know what each major involves or make any decisions about them. Afterwards, you'll review the list and compile a baseline tally of majors that interest you and that you think are worthy of further exploration.

300-Plus Majors at First Glance

	No Way	If I Had To	Don't Care	Could Be Me	Most Definitely	Comments/ Queries
	1	2	3	4	5	
Agriculture	/			|		
Agribusiness		|				
Agronomy		|				
Animal sciences				\		
Dairy sciences	\					
Equestrian studies	|					
Farm management				|		
Food science				|		
Horticulture				)		
Landscaping		|				
Soil science		\				
Architecture/Planning			/			
Architecture		|				
City/regional planning	|					
Environmental design	|					
Landscape architecture	|					
Tally number of checks on this page	5	5	1	5		

	No Way	If I Had To	Don't Care	Could Be Me	Most Definitely	Comments/ Queries
	1	**2**	**3**	**4**	**5**	
Area Studies						
African studies						
American studies						
Asian studies						
Eastern-European studies						
European studies						
French studies						
German studies						
Italian studies						
Latin-American studies						
Near-Eastern studies						
Russian studies						
Southeast-Asian studies						
Western-European studies						
Arts, Performing						
Acting						
Conducting						
Dance						
Directing (film)						
Directing (theatrical)						
Film production						
Film studies						
Music history/literature						
Music management						
Musicology/eth-nomusicology						
Music pedagogy						
Tally number of checks on this page			3	1	2	

	No Way	If I Had To	Don't Care	Could Be Me	Most Definitely	Comments/ Queries
	1	2	3	4	5	
Music performance	(					
Music theory/ composition	(					
Piano/organ	l					
Playwriting/ screenwriting	l					
Theatre arts	l					
Theatre management	\					
Voice	\					
Arts, Visual				l		
Art history	\					
Ceramics	l					
Commercial/ graphic arts					\	
Commercial photography					\	
Drawing				l		
Fashion design		\				
Illustration	l					
Industrial design					\	
Interior design				\		
Jewelry				\		
Multimedia					l	
Painting			l			
Printmaking				\		
Sculpture		\				
Studio arts		\				
Biological/Biomedical			l			
Biochemistry			l			
Biology			l			
Tally number of checks on this page	10	3	4	5	2	

	No Way	If I Had To	Don't Care	Could Be Me	Most Definitely	Comments/ Queries
	1	2	3	4	5	
Biomedical sciences				\		
Biophysics		Γ				
Biotechnology				/		
Botany				\		
Cellular/molecular biology			\			
Ecology			)			
Entomology			)			
Environmental biology			\			
Evolutionary biology				(		
Histology	/					
Marine biology				\		
Microbiology				\		
Molecular biology		\				
Plant pathology		\				
Toxicology		\				
Zoology				\		
Business		Γ				
Accounting	\					
Actuarial science	\					
Banking/financial services	\					
Business administration		\				
Business communications		(				
Business economics	\					
Business statistics	\					
E-commerce	\					
Entrepreneurship			\			
Tally number of checks on this page	7	7	5	7		

	No Way	If I Had To	Don't Care	Could Be Me	Most Definitely	Comments/ Queries
	1	2	3	4	5	
Fashion merchandising			ı			
Finance	ı					
Hospitality administration			ı			
Hospitality/recreation	ı			ı		
Hotel management				ı		
Human resources				ı		
Insurance		ı				
International business			ı			
International finance	ı					
International marketing	ı					
Labor and industrial relations		ı				
Logistics/materials management		ı				
Management information systems	ı					
Management science	ı					
Marketing	ı					
Marketing research						
Nonprofit management	ı					
Operations management	ı					
Organizational behavior	ı					
Public finance	ı					
Purchasing, procurement, and contracts	ı					
Restaurant and food services management	ı					
Tally number of checks on this page	13	3	3	2		

	No Way	If I Had To	Don't Care	Could Be Me	Most Definitely	Comments/ Queries
	1	**2**	**3**	**4**	**5**	
Sales/sales management	I					
Tourism and travel management	I					
Tourism and travel marketing	I					
Communication and Journalism			I			
Advertising				I		
Broadcast journalism			I			
Mass communication			I			
Organizational communication						
Print journalist			I			
Public relations		I				
Rhetoric	I			✓		
Computer Science and Information Technology				I		
Computer and information science			I			
Computer graphics					I	
Computer science					I	
Information science	I		I			
Information technology	I					
Networking and telecommunications	I					
Programming				I		
Systems administration	I					
Web design and development					I	
Tally number of checks on this page	8	1	5	3	3	

	No Way	If I Had To	Don't Care	Could Be Me	Most Definitely	Comments/ Queries
	1	2	3	4	5	
Education			\			
Adult and continuing education		\				
Bilingual education	\					
Counseling and guidance			\			
Curriculum and instruction		\				
Early childhood education			\			
Education administration				\		
Elementary school teaching				\		
Physical educa-tion teaching		\				
Preschool teaching	/					
Secondary school teaching	\					
Special education	/					
Speech and language disorders				\		
Subject-specific teaching			\			
Engineering				\		
Aerospace				\		
Agricultural			/			
Architectural				\		
Biomedical				\		
Ceramic		(				
Chemical		\				
Civil		(				
Tally number of checks on this page	4	6	5	7		

	No Way	If I Had To	Don't Care	Could Be Me	Most Definitely	Comments/ Queries
	1	2	3	4	5	
Computer				\		
Construction technology		l				
Drafting and design				\		
Electrical	\					
Engineering mechanics	l					
Engineering physics	l					
Engineering sciences	l					
Environmental	l					
Geological/geo-thermal	l					
Hydrological	l					
Industrial	l					
Manufacturing	l					
Marine	\					
Material science			l			
Materials		l				
Mechanical		l				
Metallurgical	l					
Mining and mineral		l				
Nuclear			l			
Operations research	\					
Optical	\					
Petroleum	\					
Robotics			l			
Software			\			
Systems	l					
Telecommunications	\					
Tally number of checks on this page	16	4	4	2		

	No Way	If I Had To	Don't Care	Could Be Me	Most Definitely	Comments/ Queries
	1	2	3	4	5	
Water quality/ waste-water treatment	I					
English Language and Literature				I		
American literature		I				
British literature		I				
Comparative literature		I				
Contemporary literature		I				
Creative writing				I		
Debate and forensics				I		
English composition		I				
Speech and rhetorical studies			I			
Technical writing	T					
Ethnic, Cultural, and Gender Studies						
African-American studies				I.		
Asian-American studies			I			
Gender studies					I	
Latino and Latina studies			I			
Native-American studies			I			
Women's studies					I	
Family, Food, Consumer, and Nutrition Sciences			I			
Child-care management	I					
Child development	\					
Tally number of checks on this page	4	5	5	4	2	

	No Way	If I Had To	Don't Care	Could Be Me	Most Definitely	Comments/ Queries
	1	**2**	**3**	**4**	**5**	
Consumer behavior						
Consumer science						
Culinary arts						
Family and community service						
Family systems						
Foods, nutrition, and wellness						
Housing studies						
Human development						
Textile and clothing studies						
Health Services and Allied Health Care						
Athletic training						
Audiology and hearing sciences						
Clinical laboratory science						
Communication disorders						
Dental hygiene						
Dietetics						
Hospital and health administration						
Laboratory technology						
Massage therapy						
Medicinal and pharmaceutical chemistry						
Nuclear medical technology						
Nursing						
Tally number of checks on this page	6	3	5	4	3	

	No Way	If I Had To	Don't Care	Could Be Me	Most Definitely	Comments/ Queries
	1	2	3	4	5	
Nursing administration						
Predental, premedical, or preveterinary studies	\					
Pharmaceutical sciences			\			
Physician's assistant		\				
Profusion sciences	\					
Radiation therapy	\					
Radiological technology	\					
Respiratory therapy	\					
Sonography	\					
History	\					
British history	\					
Contemporary history	\					
European history	\					
Medieval history	\					
Languages, Literatures, and Linguistics						
Ancient Greek	\					
Ancient Near-Eastern and biblical languages	\					
Arabic language and/or literature	\					
Chinese language and/or literature	\					
Classics	\					
Comparative literature	\					
Foreign languages and/or literature	\					
French language and/or literature	\					
Tally number of checks on this page	19	\	\	\		

	No Way	If I Had To	Don't Care	Could Be Me	Most Definitely	Comments/ Queries
	1	2	3	4	5	
German language and/or literature	ı					
Hebrew language and/or literature	ı					
Italian language and/or literature	ı					
Japanese language and/or literature	ı					
Latin	ı					
Linguistics	ı					
Modern Greek language and/or literature	ı					
Portuguese language and/or literature	ı					
Romance languages and/or literature	ı					
Scandinavian languages and/or literature	ı					
Sign language	ı					
Spanish language and literature	ı					
Law and Legal Studies						
Criminal justice	ı					
Legal administration	ı					
Legal studies	ı					
Paralegal studies	ı					
Prelaw studies	ı					
Library Science	ı					
Information sciences	ı					
Library science	ı					
Library technology	ı					
Tally number of checks on this page						

	No Way	If I Had To	Don't Care	Could Be Me	Most Definitely	Comments/ Queries
	1	2	3	4	5	
Mathematics and Statistics	I					
Actuarial studies	I					
Applied mathematics	I					
Mathematics	I					
Statistics	I					
Mental, Social, and Public Health					I	
Addiction counseling					I	
Environmental health		I				
Epidemiology	I					
Occupational health and industrial hygiene	I					
Occupational therapy	I					
Public health administration	I					
Public health education	I					
Multidisciplinary/ Interdisciplinary Studies	I					
Ancient studies	I					
Behavioral sciences			I			
Biochemistry	I					
Biological and physical sciences			I			
Biopsychology			I			
Brain and cognitive studies			I			
Entrepreneurship	I					
Gerontology	I					
Tally number of checks on this page	15	I	4		2	

	No Way	If I Had To	Don't Care	Could Be Me	Most Definitely	Comments/ Queries
	1	2	3	4	5	
Health and society			|			
Mathematics and computer science				|		
Medieval and Renaissance studies	|					
Museum studies	\					
Natural sciences	|					
Neuroscience and/or neuropsychology				|		
Nutrition sciences				|		
Peace and conflict resolution studies		|				
Science, technology, and society					|	
Systems science		|				
Natural Resources and Conservation	✓			|		
Ecology					|	
Environmental sciences					|	
Environmental studies					|	
Fishery science and/or conservation			|			
Forest sciences					|	
Forestry					|	
Natural resource management and/or policy					|	
Natural resources and conservation					|	
Wildlife/wetlands science and management					|	
Wood product technology						
Tally number of checks on this page	3	2	2	4	9	

	No Way	If I Had To	Don't Care	Could Be Me	Most Definitely	Comments/ Queries
	1	2	3	4	5	
Parks, Recreation, and Fitness				\		
Exercise science and physiology		\				
Health and physical fitness	\					
Parks, recreation, and fitness facilities management				\		
Sport management and marketing		/				
Sports and fitness administration				\		
Philosophy	(					
Argumentation	\					
Ethics	\					
Philosophy	\					
Physical Sciences					\	
Astronomy					/	
Astrophysics					\	
Atomic and molecular physics					\	
Chemical and physical oceanography					\	
Chemistry					(	
Geochemistry					\	
Geology					\	
Geophysics and seismology					\	
Organic chemistry					\	
Meteorology and atmospheric science					(	
Tally number of checks on this page	5	2		3	11	

	No Way	If I Had To	Don't Care	Could Be Me	Most Definitely	Comments/ Queries
	1	**2**	**3**	**4**	**5**	
Physics			\			
Planetary astronomy				\		
Psychology					\	
Adolescent and child psychology		\				
Behavioral psychology				\		
Clinical psychology			\			
Cognitive psychology				\		
Community psy-chology		\				
Counseling psy-chology		\				
Developmen-tal psychology		\				
Educational psy-chology			\			
Experimental psychology					\	
Industrial and organi-zational psychology				\		
Physiological psychology		\				
Psychobiology	\					
Psychology					\	
Social psychology					\	
Public Administration and Social Services	\					
Advocacy and com-munity organization	\					
Health and human services	\					
Public administration	\					
Public policy analysis	\					
Tally number of checks on this page	6	5	3	4	4	

	No Way	If I Had To	Don't Care	Could Be Me	Most Definitely	Comments/ Queries
	1	2	3	4	5	
Public and health policy			|			
Social justice				|		
Social work				|		
Religious Studies and Theological Studies	|					
Bible studies	|					
Christian studies	|		✓			
Comparative religions	|					
Islamic studies	|					
Judaic studies	|					
Pastoral counseling	|					
Preministerial, ministry, and missionary studies	|					
Rabbinical and cantor studies	|					
Religious education	|					
Sacred music	|					
Theology	|					
Youth ministry	|					
Security, Protective Services, and Justice	|					
Corrections	|					
Criminal justice	|					
Emergency response	|					
Fire protection and safety	|					
Forensic science	|					
Law enforcement	|					
Police science	|					
Tally number of checks on this page	21		1	2		

	No Way	If I Had To	Don't Care	Could Be Me	Most Definitely	Comments/ Queries
	1	2	3	4	5	
Security and protective services	1					
Security and protective technology	1					
Social Sciences	1					
Anthropology	1					
Applied economics`	1					
Archeology	1					
Criminology	1					
Economics	1					
Geography	1					
Government	1					
International relations	1					
Labor relations	1					
Social sciences				1		
Sociology				1		
Urban and regional planning				1		
Urban studies				1		
Therapy and Rehabilitation						
Art therapy				1		
Music therapy				1		
Occupational therapy		1				
Physical therapy		1				
Tally number of checks on this page	12	2		6		
Total checks on all pages	196	50	51	59	40	

Now go back over the list and jot your answers to the following questions in the spaces provided. Documenting your efforts is important as you progress from assessment to research. You won't remember your initial thoughts later, so it's best to write them down. Then you can review your notes, adding questions or revising as needed.

- How many "Most Definitely" (number 5) majors did you check? 40
- How many "Could Be Me" (number 4) majors did you check? 59
- Were you surprised at any that you identified as "Most Definitely?"
- Can you express why you find your "Most Definitely" and "Could Be Me" options interesting?
- Which majors among those you checked as "Most Definitely" or "Could Be Me" are you most curious about?

Now write your thoughts in the summary lists that follow.

My top ten first-glance majors include the following:

1. Child Psychology
2. experimental psych ?
3. addiction counseling ?
4. German? Linguistics?
5. Women's Studies
6. Creative writing ?
7. Russian /eastern european studies ?
8. _____
9. _____
10. _____

I have the following questions about these majors:

_____
_____
_____
_____

I can find answers to my questions about these majors at or from the following places or persons:

_____

_____

_____

_____

Don't leave these sections blank. You don't need to have identified ten potential majors, but you must identify at least three. Writing down some preliminary questions about these majors will start you thinking about where you might look for the answers. If you are already in college, check your school's catalog or Web site to identify which of the top ten majors listed are offered. If you're not yet in college, please check the resources of your first-choice school to see how many of the ten are offered. Next, fill in the following.

These are the prerequisites for the required courses for each of my first-glance majors:

Major 1. _____

_____

Major 2. _____

_____

Major 3. _____

_____

Major 4._____

_____

Major 5._____

_____

_____

Major 6._____

_____

_____

Major 7._____

_____

_____

Major 8._____

_____

_____

Major 9._____

_____

_____

Major 10._____

_____

_____

These are courses I have already taken (or that I can take during my first semester or quarter) that can be credited toward first-glance majors, minors, or clusters:

These are courses I can take next semester to explore, begin completing, or continue majors, minors, or clusters:

Don't worry if a particular school doesn't offer a major that interests you now. That isn't a reason to eliminate the college or university from your admissions wish list. For now, just identify similar majors. Later, when you have completed a more thorough assessment, you can determine how important a particular major might be to your academic plans.

Here are some things to think about as you review your first-glance majors:

- Have you met and spoken with someone who majored in one of these fields?
- Can you describe your top-choice majors to friends and family?
- Can you identify any typical courses that you would complete as a student in these fields?
- Can you describe these majors articulately if someone asks? If you can describe a major, you can declare that major.

The next sections provide information about the ten most popular majors in the country. Were any of these on your list?

Top Ten Majors Briefly Described

At the beginning of this book you'll find a list of the ten most popular majors as determined by data from the Department of Education National Center for Education Statistics. As you progress through your self-assessment tests and learn more about your skills and interests, you will begin to match your preferences to real majors. All of this information will help you make your ultimate decision.

If you don't find a major you're interested in among those listed below, you'll find resources cited throughout the text and in the appendices that you can use to research the subject, write your own descriptions, and identify career options related to that major.

Business

If you want to major in business, you probably want to manage people and projects, as well as develop procedures and policies. In some academic settings you'd major in business, business management, or business administration. Specialized subject fields include accounting, economics, human resources, finance, and management information systems. Concentrations or emphases can be in such fields as marketing or operations. More specialized majors, concentrations, or emphases include actuarial studies, business communication, e-commerce, entrepreneurship, fashion merchandising, hospitality, hotel, management, insurance, international, labor and industrial relations, organizational behavior, purchasing and procurement, restaurant and food management, and travel and tourism.

Foundation courses nurture skills such as identifying and resolving business and organizational problems; understanding specialized techniques used to collect and analyze data, establish strategic goals, measure effectiveness of goal-focused (profit-driven) efforts, and present findings associated with these efforts; and communicating effectively in order to achieve strategic goals. Foundation courses often include accounting, business administration, computers and information systems, finance, marketing, management, organizational behavior, and statistics, as well as complementary liberal arts, humanities, and social science classes, which can be taken as minors or clusters. In many instances, case studies, simulation, and group projects are replacing lecture-oriented instruction.

For a business major, the academic focus is on problem solving, theoretical principles, hypothesis testing, strategic planning, technology systems, and number crunching. Some students may excel at spreadsheet analysis and quantitative activities (accounting, finance, statistics), while others do better at qualitative and people-oriented jobs (marketing, personnel management, communication). Courses also explore current issues such as diversity, ethics, globalization, localization, politics, management style, and other factors that impact large and small businesses alike.

Education

In most cases, education majors are taught to teach, and they focus on learning to develop and administer curricula (lessons and units) for elementary or secondary students. Courses also address general educational topics, including developmental psychology, learning, and classroom management techniques. Other courses cover specialized topics related to student populations and the settings where teaching takes place. Specialized majors or areas of emphasis include early childhood education (prekindergarten through kindergarten), elementary education (kindergarten through sixth grade), and secondary education (grades seven through twelve), as well as special education for those with developmental and other disabilities. Student teaching experiences and subject-specific courses complement the basic courses. The latter can include English, social studies, physical education, science, or mathematics at the secondary level.

In some cases, education majors learn to counsel, advise, administer programs, and conduct research. While these areas are most often addressed in graduate school, sometimes undergraduates (specifically those completing three/two programs) will complete undergraduate prerequisites for specialized master's- or doctoral-level studies. Other educational specialties include adult and continuing education, bilingual education, educational psychology, counseling and guidance, curriculum and instruction, deaf education and American Sign Language, as well as speech and language therapy.

Typical courses taken by education majors include educational psychology, counseling, curriculum studies, multicultural issues in education, methods of teaching, history of education, and educational media.

Health Professions and Related Sciences

These majors are some of the most academically challenging but also some of the most rewarding. Majors associated with this broad category include general biological and physical sciences, health policy, and premed tracks. Premed courses include biology, general chemistry, organic chemistry, calculus, and physics. These courses establish a science grade-point average for medical schools to review, in addition to your general GPA, and they prepare students for taking the Medical College Admissions Test (MCAT). Other allied health professions, such as dental or pharmacy schools and physical therapy programs, expect students to complete these courses but not necessarily to major in traditional science fields.

While some undergraduate programs lead to certification in particular health-care fields, such as nursing, in most cases a master's degree and even doctorate are required to. Some students target their undergraduate courses on specific professions and vocations, including athletic training, audiology and speech pathology, clinical laboratory studies, dietetics, dental hygiene, hospital and health-care administration, health-care policy and public health, massage therapy, nuclear medicine, nursing, pharmacology, physical therapy, rehabilitation services, radiology technology, or respiratory therapy. Others complete general science or liberal arts undergraduate majors and a pre-health-care curriculum in preparation for graduate training.

While some schools offer a premed major, most do not. Students interested in entering medicine or related fields will complete the premed courses noted earlier but will major in other fields. All students must be prepared to complete and excel in their premed studies. They must understand and be able to apply knowledge related to the physical sciences, including biology, chemistry, anatomy, physiology, and related areas. Increasingly, social science courses, including psychology and sociology, and humanities courses, particularly those associated with philosophy and ethics, have become part of premed programs.

Psychology

Psychology majors study the mind, human behavior, animal behavior, and perception. Most undergraduates study psychology from both the social and the natural science perspectives, exploring cognition, intelligence, learning, motivation, emotion, perception, personality, physiology, brain function, and psychological disorders. Courses include general psychology, biological psychology, statistics, behavior, learning, perception, social psychology, and abnormal psychology. Some students complete specialized majors as well.

Cognitive psychology students study memory, thinking, and perception. Developmental psychology students explore psychological changes that occur throughout life. Students of experimental psychology study behavior in humans and animals, investigate motivation, cognition, attention, learning, memory, sensation, and perception. Students of industrial psychology apply psychological theories and principles to issues associated with productivity and the workplace. School psychologists assess and address the needs of students with learning or behavioral issues. Students of social psychology investigate an individual's interactions with others and apply what they learn to marketing research, organizational systems, and consulting.

Undergraduate psychology majors study a variety of theories, learn research and analytical skills, and often transition back and forth from quantitative to qualitative perspectives. The skills developed depend upon a student's particular specialization. Some students build repertoires of scientific, mathematical, and experimental design and implementation skills. Others focus on physiological and biological aspects of behavior. Others develop and build upon social science research skills or therapeutic talents.

Undergraduate degrees rarely provide the specialized skills required to perform assessment, treatment, or counseling activities. That's why many psychology undergraduates often go on to complete graduate studies that focus on clinical, counseling, developmental, experimental, industrial and organizational, school, or social psychology. Research-focused psychologists formulate and test hypotheses using a variety of testing techniques and apply statistical analysis to the data generated. Applied psychologists conduct counseling, assessment, and treatment in private practices, mental-health clinics, hospitals, and schools.

Engineering

If you're good at math and science and interested in computer-aided design, testing, and practical applications, someone may have suggested that you should study engineering. Engineering is a broad title for many specialized majors in fields that include aerospace, agriculture, architecture, biomedicine, ceramics, chemical engineering, civil engineering, computers, construction, electrical engineering, mechanics, physics, environmental engineering, geology, industry, manufacturing, marine engineering, materials, metallurgy, and mining.

Engineering students learn how to apply scientific principles to specific real-world design, manufacturing, and testing issues. They often end up working in manufacturing or research settings. As undergraduates they are equally comfortable whether in the lab or on project teams, drafting plans or testing hypotheses, doing solo research or making presentations. In all these contexts they are quantitatively driven and analytically strong. They are fundamentally scientists. Engineering majors are motivated and multifaceted students who face demanding curricula but are rewarded with a broad array of career paths from which to choose.

Visual and Performing Arts

Visual arts majors focus on either fine arts or graphic arts. Graphic arts majors learn to apply their talents to commercial projects in advertising, design, retail, publishing, and related fields. They take courses related to the design and creation of packaging, advertising, promotional displays, brochures, illustrations, magazines, books, logos, stationery, storyboards for ads and video productions, Web design, video game design, and product design. They work on projects independently or in groups in order to produce a body of work called a portfolio. Today, graphic design entails the use of computers, cameras, and printers in addition to pencils, pens, and paper.

Fine arts majors study and create in media as diverse as painting, sculpture, ceramics, and fabric. They express themselves as artists, sculptors, printmakers, designers, photographers, and sketch artists. Like their graphic-art counterparts, fine arts majors also assemble a portfolio of representative work. Majors complete projects that are reviewed, analyzed, and critiqued. Talents and career goals vary from student to student. Courses include color theory, art history, figure drawing, graphic design, electronic art, typography, painting, and mixed media.

In addition to selling work in galleries, post-baccalaureate specializations for fine art majors include education, communication media, publishing, museum curatorships, and art therapy.

Performing arts majors express and nurture their talents in courses and specializations associated with drama, literature, film, and music. Courses include acting; theater history; instrumental or vocal performance; stage direction, lighting, and management; scriptwriting; improvisation; technical production; and movement. These majors share a passion for performance. In addition to class work, they perform in college, community, and other types of productions. Performing arts majors become actors, dancers, members of orchestras or other musical groups, singers, directors, television and radio personalities, producers, and filmmakers.

Computer and Information Sciences

Computer science majors study mathematics and science and specialize in many diverse areas. They are detail-oriented, creative problem solvers. In general, they explore information technologies, programming, and the application of computers and electronic devices within the business, education, and health care industries, as well as other contexts.

Programming involves writing, testing, and maintaining the software code that instructs computer hardware to perform specific functions. Information science involves developing systems to store, retrieve, and analyze data needed to complete various tasks. Students must be able to understand theory as well as practical applications.

Specialties include software development, language recognition, robotics, artificial intelligence, and hardware design. Majors and emphases include information systems, information technology, networking and telecommunications, programming, system design and administration, Web design, and software and hardware architecture. Courses include circuits, algorithms, programming, systems design and analysis, operating systems, and artificial intelligence. Coursework involves the completion of many projects, both individually and in groups. Computer science students are often by nature independent thinkers, but they must be able to collaborate with others to solve problems.

Liberal Arts and Sciences, General Studies, and Humanities

Liberal arts majors include, but aren't limited to, economics, English, history, political science, mathematics, history, languages, and the arts. More broadly defined, they can also include the natural sciences, social sciences, humanities, archeology, and anthropology.

If you want to study business, but your college doesn't offer that major, economics may be as close as you can get. This course of study investigates how individuals, businesses, governments, and other entities allocate resources like time, money, and manpower. It also examines the way resources, goods, and services are produced, allocated, and consumed. Courses include statistics, econometrics, macroeconomics, microeconomics, labor economics, money, credit and banking, wage and price theory, and research methodologies. Quantitative skills are developed through exercises, models, case studies, courses, and assignments.

Majors apply economic policy in areas like finance, labor, agriculture, transportation, energy, durable goods, manufactured goods, and health care. Some students focus on issues related to unemployment, inflation, prices, wages, and interest rates. They conduct and examine research, analyze data, identify and monitor trends, and seek to forecast the impact of trends on the availability or price associated with specific resources, products, financial markets, and interest rates.

English majors focus on the English language, literature, and writing. They study contemporary and historical works of fiction, nonfiction, poetry, prose, and drama. They review and analyze the works of others and may also write essays, novels, short stories, or plays. Courses and related specialties include American literature, British literature, comparative literature, creative writing, debate and forensics, composition, speech and rhetoric, technical writing, literary criticism, and drama. Some majors may specialize in the writing of a specific author, such as Shakespeare or James Joyce, or on a specific genre.

History majors study the past to understand how individuals, cultures, governments, and societies behaved. Often they apply insights gained from studying history to current issues in order to compare historical and contemporary contexts. Courses can include Western civilization, Russian history, American history, medieval history, and modern history. Students who choose this major conduct research using a variety of sources, including unpublished writing, publications, online resources, and oral histories. Most majors choose a specific geopolitical region, time period, culture, or other specialized subject as their focus.

Political science majors study politics and government through both qualitative and quantitative research, including statistical analyses of issues, trends, and budgetary data. Courses include politics and religion, statistics, legislative processes, the presidency, comparative government, foreign policy, political philosophy, international political economics, and research methods. Areas of study include political parties and processes; law and justice; elections; local, state, and federal governmental systems; legislation; revolutions, public policy, and international relations. Majors develop skills in research, analysis, critical thinking, argumentation, and communication.

They may seek careers in government, but many go to law school or into journalism.

Mathematics majors take courses in calculus, statistics, differential equations, linear algebra, abstract algebra, numbers theory, geometry, and complex variables. They can complete problem sets, proofs, and other mathematical problems. Some mathematics majors go into business as actuaries, analysts, or auditors, while others use their skills in education, government, and other areas.

Language majors seek to understand and converse using a second or third nonnative language. Most college students were once required to study Greek and Latin, but today most study modern European languages, including French, Spanish, Italian, German, and Portuguese. Increasingly, students now also nurture fluency in Japanese, Chinese, Russian, and Arabic. Language study often includes the study of other cultures, customs, and literature. Teaching is the obvious career option for some language majors, but a second language can be combined with other courses of study. Thus, majoring in a language can easily translate to a career in business, statistics, education, or communication. Language majors can build careers in international business, media, communications, and government, as well as other areas.

Multidisciplinary/Interdisciplinary Studies

Multidisciplinary and interdisciplinary majors study two or more related subject areas at the same time. Majors can include ancient studies; behavioral sciences; biochemistry, brain, and cognitive studies; health and society; mathematics and computer studies; neuroscience and neuropsychology; and systems science. Blending majors, minors, clusters, and certificates is one recommended way to approach interdisciplinary and multidisciplinary studies. Some students create their own majors, an option offered by almost all colleges and universities.

Behavioral science majors blend psychology, sociology, and biology to investigate human behavior. These students become trained scientists, researchers, and facilitators, with careers in health care, education, human services, government, social work, and therapy. Peace-and-conflict-resolution majors approach their studies from historical, political, economic, sociological, and perhaps religious perspectives. They too can build careers in education, as well as government and law.

Interdisciplinary and multidisciplinary studies can go beyond titles, and career connections might involve some creative thinking. Blending majors, minors, clusters, and certificates is a way to complete studies in this category, and this approach is highly recommended.

Protective Services

These multidisciplinary majors combine the social and behavioral sciences with criminal justice and law-enforcement subjects to address issues related to crime, terrorism, drug abuse, incarceration, and rehabilitation. Courses include legal procedures, criminology, civil liability, security management, police strategy, evidence, juvenile justice, and incarceration policies and history. Students complete these majors in preparation for careers in law enforcement; corrections, parole, and probation; private investigation; and law.

Beginning to Focus

You have begun the assessment and research necessary to decide on a major. Guided by your values and interests, you have noted your initial reactions to a list of possible majors and produced your list of first-glance majors. You have reviewed the descriptions of what's involved in some of these majors and have probably started thinking about your options. Does one major look particularly interesting? Were you surprised by anything you read? Was it easier to begin the process than you expected?

As you complete the tests in the following chapters, you will begin to understand more about yourself and your interests. You will also develop strategies and goals and move closer to choosing a major. Relax, and have fun!

Chapter 3

Common Questions and Issues about Majors

The French anthropologist Claude Lévi-Strauss once wrote, "The scientific mind does not so much provide the right answers as ask the right questions." You will find that answering a series of targeted questions can help you pinpoint the major that's right for you. As you work through this book, you will find that there are no right answers; there are only the answers that are right for *you*—your circumstances, interests, values, and talents.

3

College Major Common Questions Test

In this chapter, you will be asked to answer some questions and to think about your answers. Perhaps you have wondered about some of these topics. As you review your answers, you will see that some questions were harder for you to answer clearly, indicating a need for further reflection or research. Later, you will list courses you have taken in high school and those you might take in college and think about how they correlate with your initial thoughts about a major.

To begin the Common Questions Test, read each question and rate its significance to you by circling a number between 1 and 10. A rating of 1 is the lowest end of the scale, indicating the question is of "little personal significance." A low rating also might indicate that you are confident you know the correct answer to the question. A rating of 10 indicates that the question covers an area of great interest to you, probably because you know the question is important but have never been able to figure out a good answer: "I've asked this question many times and have long wanted an answer." The ratings in the middle indicate shades of interest. Choose numbers at the low end of the scale for questions of relatively little interest (that is, questions you're pretty sure you have answered), and circle higher numbers if you find a question more interesting, important, or confusing.

Common Questions Test

Questions	Score
Do I choose a college before a major, or a major before a college?	1 2 3 4 5 6 7 8 9 10
How do I choose or "declare" a major?	1 2 3 4 5 6 7 8 9 10
Do majors really matter, academically or otherwise?	1 2 3 4 5 6 7 8 9 10
Do employers really care about my major?	1 2 3 4 5 6 7 8 9 10
Do graduate and professional schools really care about my major?	1 2 3 4 5 6 7 8 9 10
What if I change my mind about my major?	1 2 3 4 5 6 7 8 9 10
What will be the consequences if it takes me more than four years to graduate?	1 2 3 4 5 6 7 8 9 10

How do I plan or prepare for graduate or professional school?	1 2 3 4 5 6 7 8 9 10
What about dual degrees, minors, and certificates?	1 2 3 4 5 6 7 8 9 10
What do I do if I want to major in something parents or friends consider impractical?	1 2 3 4 5 6 7 8 9 10
How can I predict whether the major and career I choose will be in demand, both when I graduate and after?	1 2 3 4 5 6 7 8 9 10
Can I break into a field some might consider not related to my major?	1 2 3 4 5 6 7 8 9 10
TOTALS	1 2 3 4 5 6 7 8 9 10
Tally the number of questions with each score	

Once you have noted your answers, identify those you rated with an 8 or above. These are the questions you need to answer immediately. Perhaps you have to declare a major very soon. Maybe your parents are impatient to get a decision about a major from you, or you just like to plan well ahead. Identify the five questions that are most significant to you and write them in order of importance in the spaces below, with the most important first.

1. _____

2. _____

3. _____

4. _____

5. _____

Next, review the questions and contemplate your answers. Do you have any ideas or opinions? Jot down a brief first impression answer for each question. The following sections provide answers to all the questions in the test. Review these answers and compare them to your own.

1. _____

2. _____

3. _____

4. _____

5. _____

Common Question #1

Do I choose a college before a major, or a major before a college?

It's best to identify your college first, then your major, unless you have very specialized goals and there are only a few schools that offer majors related to those goals. You base your decision on what school to attend on many factors. One of those factors—but not the only one—is what majors are offered. Other factors include the curriculum (required courses), specialized programs (such as overseas studies, co-ops, and internships), the campus environment, selectivity and reputation of the institution, availability of research experiences, family or personal finances, and intangibles associated with your vision of your education. Can you envision yourself happy and productive at this institution for four or more years? If you've selected a school based on a particular major and your interest in that major wanes, your attachment to that institution might flag as well. If you use broader criteria and the school offers several majors of interest to you, you could more easily address any future change of heart.

Some students do focus on careers and related majors first, and then they identify schools that offer programs in their chosen field. If you have a specific major or career in mind, you can conduct research to identify whether more than one major can lead to the same career goals. If your goals involve very specialized academic requirements, you will need to research the best academic programs offered by various institutions.

Common Question #2

How do I choose or "declare" a major?

While each school is different, declaring a major at almost any institution is as easy as filling out a form. Most require that a faculty or professional advisor approve your major after analyzing the necessary prerequisite courses, courses you have completed and those you have yet to take, as well as your academic status. The declaration isn't difficult; it's the choosing that is fraught with so much frustration and procrastination. You will be able to choose a major after completing the assessments and research outlined in this book. It's easy to change majors, too, so keep an open mind regarding how long it might take to complete your undergraduate studies in your chosen major.

Common Question #3

Do majors really matter, academically or otherwise?

Yes. The major you choose will influence your choice of courses and when you take them. In most cases, you will take at least eight to twelve courses related to your major. You will be spending hours attending lectures, seminars, and labs; reading; conducting research; and discussing issues related to that subject.

It helps if the major is something that truly interests you. Don't choose a particular major because you think it will guarantee career or internship success. Remember that the most selective schools are liberal arts oriented and offer majors that are general rather than vocational. While majoring in certain subjects does make it easier to find some internships and jobs related to specific fields, a better plan would be to complete the assessment of your goals and interests, research your options and school choices, and choose a major in a subject related to your academic and career interests. Once you have clearly articulated your goals, you will have a better idea of what to major in, and you can then supplement that major with a minor, a cluster, or a few specialized courses.

Common Question #4

Do employers really care about my major?

Some employers do focus recruiting efforts on particular majors, such as various engineering disciplines, but others recruit from a variety of majors. The latter group is concerned more with a candidate's qualifications and motivation than any particular area of study. A firm that wants to hire an accountant, for instance, might look at many applicants, many of whom majored in subjects other than accounting, as long as they took the requisite accounting courses. As you complete your research on the various majors of interest to you, you will learn which employers are more interested in majors and which are more concerned about applicants with internships, projects, or other skill-building experiences. This knowledge will help you focus your efforts on supplemental courses, if necessary.

In years past, when there were fewer college graduates, employers were willing to view candidates based on potential rather then specific major-connected qualifications. Today, with well over a million students completing undergraduate studies annually and fewer jobs available, employers can be more major-focused. Employers do care about majors, but they also care about goal articulation—in other words, how well a student's course of study prepared him or her for a chosen career. In today's economy, employers look for connections between majors and careers and require that candidates express goals clearly and concisely.

Common Question #5

Do graduate and professional schools really care about my major?

Not necessarily. In most cases, professional schools offering advanced degrees in law, medicine, nursing, engineering, business require you to complete specific prerequisite courses, or courses that develop particular skills and perspectives, but they don't necessarily require a particular major. However if you intend to pursue graduate study immediately after college in a subject-specific master's or doctoral program, your major does matter.

Law schools do not require completion of any specific majors. But they do look for the capacity to conduct research, identify precedent, and document findings in special formats. Medical and nursing schools require a set of specific science courses and labs and the ability to use investigative qualities in laboratory and clinical contexts. Business schools accept applicants who have completed varied majors, but they do look for overall quantitative as well as qualitative skills.

While it is most likely too early for you to think about graduate study, research will uncover whether additional studies are required to enter or excel within particular careers. Do you think graduate study is in your future? Do you know what majors or courses would enhance your chances to be admitted to graduate school? Do you know what resources are needed to uncover graduate-school options?

Common Question #6

What if I change my mind about my major?

Changing majors at most schools is quite easy. Too many students exaggerate the importance—or finality—of choosing a major, so they delay making the choice in the first place. You can always change your mind, whatever the major you declare.

Bear in mind that changing your major may affect the length of time it takes to complete all the required courses, so this should be taken into account when making your decision. Still, it's your prerogative to change your mind. If the new major is the one that you feel passionate about, then it's worth whatever investment of time is needed to switch.

Summer can be a good time to explore major alternatives, when you can take a course or two to test newly discovered interests. Taking a few courses at a local community college or state institution can be an economic and effective bridge to a new major. Also, if credits are transferable to your current school, you can change majors and still graduate within four years.

Common Question #7

What will be the consequences if it takes me more than four years to graduate?

Most undergraduates finish college within four years, but for many students it takes more time to complete all the required courses for a major. In fact, at some state institutions, particularly public schools with high enrollments, the average time to graduate is more than four years. Don't let others' expectations influence your decision. While your parents may care about the extra time because of the additional expense, employers and graduate programs don't.

Common Question #8

How do I plan or prepare for graduate or professional school?

Graduate and professional schools are not, like undergraduate schools, exploratory in nature. In other words, you apply only after completing research and gaining focus—when you have a clear career goal in mind and know exactly why you need this advanced degree. Don't apply to graduate school because you can't think of career options or alternatives.

Graduate schools are best for those who are focused and recognize that additional studies are critical steps on the path to academic and career success. Applying to a graduate or professional school should be done as an expression of your career focus. Follow your heart, but don't forget to use your head. Be honest with yourself as you research specific academic subjects, preprofessional training, and specialized skills building associated with graduate and professional schools.

Common Question #9

What about dual degrees, minors, and certificates?

There are many advantages to pursuing a second major, adding a minor or cluster, or earning a certificate. Taking several additional courses outside of your major can help you enter a particular career field or graduate school. Three or more courses in a particular subject area can serve to enhance your confidence and add the competence you need to achieve your post-baccalaureate goals. You don't need to take these courses at the school from which you earn your degree. Instead, you might choose to earn a specialized certificate or take supplemental courses inexpensively at a community college or state institution during the summer while you complete your major elsewhere. Certificates can qualify you for such jobs as an emergency medical technician, a respiratory therapist, or a paralegal. A few courses in such things as journalism, grant writing, education, or marketing can add employability to any major.

Common Question #10

What do I do if I want to major in something my parents or friends consider impractical?

The perceived practicality of a subject area is highly personal and subjective. While some people might consider philosophy, religious studies, or art history impractical in terms of the likelihood that you will eventually find a job in the field, their argument is baseless and easily refuted with a little research. As you will discover as you work through this book and explore various majors, any field of study can lead to a rewarding and fulfilling career. The key is to identify your specific and realistic goals regarding your chosen major, connect those goals to career options, and apply yourself to your academic pursuits. Your ability to explain your plans and your commitment in clear language will go far in allaying your parents' concerns. Also, don't forget the value of a minor or a dual major (as discussed in the answer to the previous question). Sometimes all you need to achieve the appearance of practicality—even to your parents—is to supplement your major with a certificate or a few career-oriented courses to fit your subject area to a job.

Common Question #11

How can I predict whether the major and career I choose will be in demand, both when I graduate and after?

You can't. It's impossible to predict the supply-and-demand process in the job world. There are statistics available that indicate the popularity of various professions by state or in the country, but in the long run it will be your academic achievements, confidence, and competence that will attract employers. You can't control the economic factors, but the more internships and other resume-building projects you complete, the more successful your job search or graduate-school applications will be.

You cannot predict demand for specific majors, or for candidates applying for particular jobs. But if you choose majors wisely based upon self-knowledge, you can enhance your chances for success. No matter your major, maximize your effort and earn the best grades possible. Focus on factors you can control and on those that enhance your taking confident steps on your path to academic and career achievement.

Common Question #12

Can I break into a field some might consider not related to my major?

Maybe. If you know what field you're interested in and the skills required to enter it, then you can supplement your major with a targeted minor, cluster, certificate, or one-course-at-a-time strategy. It may take only one course or half a dozen to enhance your candidacy; regardless, the effort will probably be well worth it.

Courses that require the completion of projects, not just papers and exams, can be reflected effectively on a resume. Explore internship programs, such as the Washington Center Program (*www.twc.edu*) or the University of Dreams (*www.uofdreams.com*). For a fee, such programs provide housing, internships, seminars, and other valuable experiences. Whatever you do, don't just try to convince employers you have "potential." In this case your actions—taking courses or completing projects or internships—will speak much more loudly than words.

A few goal-specific courses, completed before or after you graduate, can make you a very attractive candidate in almost any career field. Majors can reflect academic curiosities, and minors or clusters can reveal career strategies.

High School and College Reflective/ Projective Transcripts

While much of the decision-making about majors involves assessing personal criteria, it also involves an understanding of academic issues. Complement your self-knowledge with an understanding of your past academic performance, intellectual interests, and a sense of those subjects in which you excel.

This next exercise asks you to identify the secondary and college courses that you have completed to date and to note your thoughts about how they might impact your choice of major. You will also list courses that you may take in the future, identifying the key concepts covered in each. The act of inventorying and analyzing your academic history, as well as thinking about your future academic career, should help you become more aware of your options. It will also increase your confidence in your choices.

High School Reflective Transcript

Think about courses you completed in high school. Which did you
enjoy the most, and why? Which did you do well in?

Use this form to list the top twenty courses you completed in high school. These are the courses you found most interesting and most inspiring, as well as those you earned high grades in. Briefly describe the concepts, topics, and themes that were covered in these classes. Last, based upon your initial impressions, cite the implications these courses have on your choice of major.

Courses Taken	Key Concepts and Themes Covered	Major Implications

College Reflective Transcript

Think about the courses you have completed in college so far. Which did
you enjoy the most, and why? Which did you do well in?

List the top courses you have completed in college. These are the courses you found most interesting and most inspiring, as well as those you earned high grades in. Briefly describe the concepts, topics, and themes that were covered in these classes. Last, based upon your initial impressions, cite the implications these courses have on your choice of major.

Courses Taken	Key Concepts and Themes Covered	Major Implications

College Projective Transcript

With your prospective majors in mind, think about the courses you would like to take in college.

Identify the top courses you would like to complete in college. These are the courses you think you'll find most interesting. Briefly list the concepts, topics, and themes that are covered in these classes. Cite some implications that these courses might have on your choice of major.

Courses to Be Taken	Key Concepts and Themes to Be Covered	Major Implications

Study the list on your two reflective transcripts (from high school and college) and answer the following questions:

- Do you see a relationship among the courses you have already taken and your list of first-glance majors?
- Do you see any patterns developing? In particular, do you tend to take particular types of courses (such as science, math, language, or literature)?
- Do you excel at certain types of courses (for instance, labs, writing, or theoretical)?

Now look at your projective transcript. Review your list of first-glance majors and the course offerings at your school (or prospective schools) and do the following:

1. Check the classes you have listed against departmental requirements. Identify which are prerequisites for a major of interest to you and which would satisfy course requirements.
2. Circle or highlight any courses that satisfy requirements for more than one of your first-glance majors.
3. List the top ten "must take" courses (using titles, not just course numbers). This list includes any courses identified in step two. If there were none, list the classes from your projective transcript according to their order of importance to you.

If you're already in college, you may have completed a similar exercise before selecting courses for the semester or quarter. If you're a high school student, this may be the first time you have tried thinking so far ahead. It may seem a bit difficult at first, but it's important. The more you learn how to connect your past successes and interests to future courses and possible majors, the easier your decision-making will be down the road.

Questions about Majors

You are well on your way to completing the research you need. As you gather the answers to these and other questions, you will begin to accumulate the knowledge and build the confidence that will help you develop an academic strategy, choose a major, and ultimately find a job. In the next chapter you'll continue your self-assessment by exploring your opinions about academics, work style, and your readiness to declare a major. Before that, though, here are some sample questions you might want to ask as you conduct the research needed to begin to focus on a major:

- What courses are required of the majors I am thinking about?
- Have I already completed prerequisite and required courses related to any majors I am contemplating?
- What courses have I done well in? Why?
- What courses have I found challenging? Why?
- Can I complete the courses required for my major and earn a grade-point average above 3.0?
- What career fields are associated with the majors that interest me?
- What courses can I take, in addition to those required by my major, to qualify me for career fields that interest me?

Here are a few questions to ask as you talk to people who have completed majors in subjects that interest you:

- Why did you choose your major?
- What were the most rewarding, easiest, most demanding, and most useful courses you took?
- If you could go back to college, would you take any other courses?
- How did you get this job or into this field?
- How did you get your first job in this field?
- Does your job require specialized education or graduate training?
- In addition to taking courses related to my major, what else should I do to prepare myself for a job of this kind?
- Can you suggest a few other people I could talk to about their academic experiences?

Chapter 4
Know Thyself

The British philosopher F. H. Bradley once noted, "The one self-knowledge worth having is to know one's own mind." Only with a real understanding of your values, interests, and skills, along with a comprehension of how those meld with various career alternatives, can you prioritize your options and make constructive decisions about your major and, by extension, your future. With this chapter you'll begin your examination of *you* through a series of revealing true-false tests.

4

Test Your Self-Awareness

This true-false test is part of the assessment step in your ARM strategy. It's designed to help you learn more about how you feel about some majors and careers, as well as the whole research and decision-making process. You may learn some things about yourself that you didn't know before. The test should inspire you to continue researching majors and careers. Later, you'll also begin to learn about some effective research techniques and tools, including publications, interviews, and Web sites.

Answering a series of true-false statements can sometimes produce a surprising amount of information. The key is to answer spontaneously and truthfully. Don't overthink your responses or try to second-guess the test. Later, you'll combine your assessment of this test with that of the other tests and begin to develop a clearer picture of the major that's right for you.

This test has two steps. First, read each question and answer "true" or "false." After you complete the test, you will come back and mark each response on the true-false continuum.

True-False Test of Self-Awareness

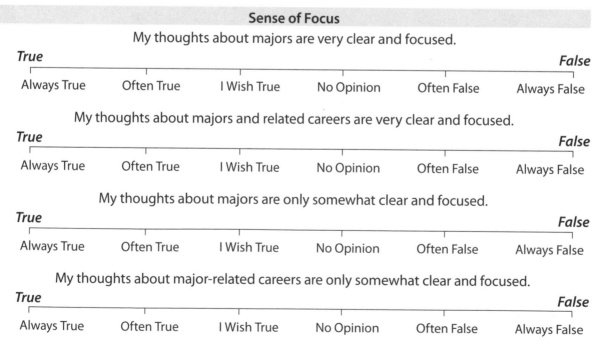

Sense of Focus

My thoughts about majors are very clear and focused.

True					False
Always True	Often True	I Wish True	No Opinion	Often False	Always False

My thoughts about majors and related careers are very clear and focused.

True					False
Always True	Often True	I Wish True	No Opinion	Often False	Always False

My thoughts about majors are only somewhat clear and focused.

True					False
Always True	Often True	I Wish True	No Opinion	Often False	Always False

My thoughts about major-related careers are only somewhat clear and focused.

True					False
Always True	Often True	I Wish True	No Opinion	Often False	Always False

My thoughts about majors are rather vague and unfocused.

True   *False*

| Always True | Often True | I Wish True | No Opinion | Often False | Always False |

My thoughts about major-related careers are rather vague and unfocused.

True   *False*

| Always True | Often True | I Wish True | No Opinion | Often False | Always False |

I am very confused, anxious, and concerned about majors.

True   *False*

| Always True | Often True | I Wish True | No Opinion | Often False | Always False |

I am very confused, anxious, and concerned about major-related careers.

True   *False*

| Always True | Often True | I Wish True | No Opinion | Often False | Always False |

Academic Interests

I am curious about exploring majors associated with agriculture.

True   *False*

| Always True | Often True | I Wish True | No Opinion | Often False | Always False |

I am curious about exploring majors associated with architecture/planning.

True   *False*

| Always True | Often True | I Wish True | No Opinion | Often False | Always False |

I am curious about exploring majors associated with area studies.

True   *False*

| Always True | Often True | I Wish True | No Opinion | Often False | Always False |

I am curious about exploring majors associated with fine and performing arts.

True   *False*

| Always True | Often True | I Wish True | No Opinion | Often False | Always False |

I am curious about exploring majors associated with biological and biomedical sciences.

True   *False*

| Always True | Often True | I Wish True | No Opinion | Often False | Always False |

I am curious about exploring majors associated with business.

True   *False*

| Always True | Often True | I Wish True | No Opinion | Often False | Always False |

I am curious about exploring majors associated with communication and journalism.

True   *False*

| Always True | Often True | I Wish True | No Opinion | Often False | Always False |

I am curious about exploring majors associated with computer science and information technology.

True   *False*

| Always True | Often True | I Wish True | No Opinion | Often False | Always False |

I am curious about exploring majors associated with education.

True   *False*

| Always True | Often True | I Wish True | No Opinion | Often False | Always False |

I am curious about exploring majors associated with engineering.

True   *False*

| Always True | Often True | I Wish True | No Opinion | Often False | Always False |

I am curious about exploring majors associated with English language and literature.

True   *False*

| Always True | Often True | I Wish True | No Opinion | Often False | Always False |

I am curious about exploring majors associated with ethnic, cultural, and gender studies.

True   *False*

| Always True | Often True | I Wish True | No Opinion | Often False | Always False |

I am curious about exploring majors associated with family, food,
consumer and nutrition sciences.

True   *False*

| Always True | Often True | I Wish True | No Opinion | Often False | Always False |

I am curious about exploring majors associated with health services and allied health care.

True   *False*

| Always True | Often True | I Wish True | No Opinion | Often False | Always False |

I am curious about exploring majors associated with languages, literatures, and linguistics.

True   *False*

| Always True | Often True | I Wish True | No Opinion | Often False | Always False |

I am curious about exploring majors associated with law and legal studies.

True   *False*

| Always True | Often True | I Wish True | No Opinion | Often False | Always False |

I am curious about exploring majors associated with library science.

True   *False*

| Always True | Often True | I Wish True | No Opinion | Often False | Always False |

I am curious about exploring majors associated with mathematics and statistics.

True   *False*

| Always True | Often True | I Wish True | No Opinion | Often False | Always False |

I am curious about exploring majors associated with mental, social, and public health.

True   *False*

| Always True | Often True | I Wish True | No Opinion | Often False | Always False |

I am curious about exploring majors associated with multidisciplinary/interdisciplinary studies.

True   *False*

| Always True | Often True | I Wish True | No Opinion | Often False | Always False |

I am curious about exploring majors associated with natural resources and conservation.

True   *False*

| Always True | Often True | I Wish True | No Opinion | Often False | Always False |

I am curious about exploring majors associated with parks, recreation, and fitness.

True   *False*

| Always True | Often True | I Wish True | No Opinion | Often False | Always False |

I am curious about exploring majors associated with philosophy.

True   *False*

| Always True | Often True | I Wish True | No Opinion | Often False | Always False |

I am curious about exploring majors associated with psychology.

True   *False*

| Always True | Often True | I Wish True | No Opinion | Often False | Always False |

I am curious about exploring majors associated with religious studies and theological studies.

True   *False*

| Always True | Often True | I Wish True | No Opinion | Often False | Always False |

I am curious about exploring majors associated with security, protective services, and justice.

True   *False*

| Always True | Often True | I Wish True | No Opinion | Often False | Always False |

I am curious about exploring majors associated with social sciences.

True   *False*

| Always True | Often True | I Wish True | No Opinion | Often False | Always False |

I am curious about exploring majors associated with therapy and rehabilitation.

True   *False*

| Always True | Often True | I Wish True | No Opinion | Often False | Always False |

Career Interests

I am curious about exploring careers associated with agriculture.

True   *False*

| Always True | Often True | I Wish True | No Opinion | Often False | Always False |

I am curious about exploring careers associated with architecture/planning.

True   *False*

| Always True | Often True | I Wish True | No Opinion | Often False | Always False |

I am curious about exploring careers associated with area studies.

True   *False*

| Always True | Often True | I Wish True | No Opinion | Often False | Always False |

I am curious about exploring careers associated with fine and performing arts.

True   *False*

| Always True | Often True | I Wish True | No Opinion | Often False | Always False |

I am curious about exploring careers associated with biological and biomedical sciences.

True   *False*

| Always True | Often True | I Wish True | No Opinion | Often False | Always False |

I am curious about exploring careers associated with business.

True   *False*

| Always True | Often True | I Wish True | No Opinion | Often False | Always False |

I am curious about exploring careers associated with communication and journalism.

True   *False*

| Always True | Often True | I Wish True | No Opinion | Often False | Always False |

I am curious about exploring careers associated with
computer science and information technology.

True   *False*

| Always True | Often True | I Wish True | No Opinion | Often False | Always False |

I am curious about exploring careers associated with education.

True   *False*

| Always True | Often True | I Wish True | No Opinion | Often False | Always False |

I am curious about exploring careers associated with engineering.

True   *False*

| Always True | Often True | I Wish True | No Opinion | Often False | Always False |

I am curious about exploring careers associated with English language and literature.

True   *False*

| Always True | Often True | I Wish True | No Opinion | Often False | Always False |

I am curious about exploring careers associated with ethnic, cultural, and gender studies.

True   *False*

| Always True | Often True | I Wish True | No Opinion | Often False | Always False |

I am curious about exploring careers associated with
family, food, consumer and nutrition sciences.

True   *False*

Always True	Often True	I Wish True	No Opinion	Often False	Always False

I am curious about exploring careers associated with health services and allied health care.

True   *False*

Always True	Often True	I Wish True	No Opinion	Often False	Always False

I am curious about exploring careers associated with languages, literatures, and linguistics.

True   *False*

Always True	Often True	I Wish True	No Opinion	Often False	Always False

I am curious about exploring careers associated with law and legal studies.

True   *False*

Always True	Often True	I Wish True	No Opinion	Often False	Always False

I am curious about exploring careers associated with library science.

True   *False*

Always True	Often True	I Wish True	No Opinion	Often False	Always False

I am curious about exploring careers associated with mathematics and statistics.

True   *False*

Always True	Often True	I Wish True	No Opinion	Often False	Always False

I am curious about exploring careers associated with mental, social, and public health.

True   *False*

Always True	Often True	I Wish True	No Opinion	Often False	Always False

I am curious about exploring careers associated with multidisciplinary/interdisciplinary studies.

True   *False*

Always True	Often True	I Wish True	No Opinion	Often False	Always False

I am curious about exploring careers associated with natural resources and conservation.

True   *False*

Always True	Often True	I Wish True	No Opinion	Often False	Always False

I am curious about exploring careers associated with parks, recreation, and fitness.

True   *False*

| Always True | Often True | I Wish True | No Opinion | Often False | Always False |

I am curious about exploring careers associated with philosophy.

True   *False*

| Always True | Often True | I Wish True | No Opinion | Often False | Always False |

I am curious about exploring careers associated with psychology.

True   *False*

| Always True | Often True | I Wish True | No Opinion | Often False | Always False |

I am curious about exploring careers associated with religious studies and theological studies.

True   *False*

| Always True | Often True | I Wish True | No Opinion | Often False | Always False |

I am curious about exploring careers associated with security, protective services, and justice.

True   *False*

| Always True | Often True | I Wish True | No Opinion | Often False | Always False |

I am curious about exploring careers associated with social sciences.

True   *False*

| Always True | Often True | I Wish True | No Opinion | Often False | Always False |

I am curious about exploring careers associated with therapy and rehabilitation.

True   *False*

| Always True | Often True | I Wish True | No Opinion | Often False | Always False |

Major Assessment and Research

I have taken a major assessment and it was very helpful.

True   *False*

| Always True | Often True | I Wish True | No Opinion | Often False | Always False |

I have taken a major assessment and it was not very helpful.

True   *False*

| Always True | Often True | I Wish True | No Opinion | Often False | Always False |

I have read a publication that discussed my major and it was very helpful.

True   *False*

| Always True | Often True | I Wish True | No Opinion | Often False | Always False |

I have read a major publication and it was not very helpful.

True   *False*

| Always True | Often True | I Wish True | No Opinion | Often False | Always False |

I have completed an informal major exercise and it was very helpful.

True   *False*

| Always True | Often True | I Wish True | No Opinion | Often False | Always False |

I have completed an informal major exercise and it was not very helpful.

True   *False*

| Always True | Often True | I Wish True | No Opinion | Often False | Always False |

I know my Myers-Briggs Code and feel it can help major decision-making.

True   *False*

| Always True | Often True | I Wish True | No Opinion | Often False | Always False |

I know my Holland code and feel it can help major decision-making.

True   *False*

| Always True | Often True | I Wish True | No Opinion | Often False | Always False |

I understand the ARM model and feel it can help major decision-making.

True   *False*

| Always True | Often True | I Wish True | No Opinion | Often False | Always False |

I know where I can receive academic advising counseling for major decision-making.

True   *False*

| Always True | Often True | I Wish True | No Opinion | Often False | Always False |

I know where I can find research resources associated with major decision-making.

True   *False*

| Always True | Often True | I Wish True | No Opinion | Often False | Always False |

I have used one or two helpful major decision-making research resources.

True   *False*

| Always True | Often True | I Wish True | No Opinion | Often False | Always False |

Major Decision Making

I have self-imposed deadlines or other deadlines for choosing my major.

True   *False*

| Always True | Often True | I Wish True | No Opinion | Often False | Always False |

I must choose my major very, very soon.

True   *False*

| Always True | Often True | I Wish True | No Opinion | Often False | Always False |

I have significant concerns about choosing a major, so I want to avoid it as long as possible.

True   *False*

| Always True | Often True | I Wish True | No Opinion | Often False | Always False |

I understand that my major decision is tentative, and it can be changed.

True   *False*

| Always True | Often True | I Wish True | No Opinion | Often False | Always False |

Major Influences

I have positive major role models, individuals who successfully completed majors of interest.

True   *False*

| Always True | Often True | I Wish True | No Opinion | Often False | Always False |

I have positive career role models, individuals who completed
majors of interest and entered targeted career fields.

True   *False*

| Always True | Often True | I Wish True | No Opinion | Often False | Always False |

My parents have said they will support me forever, so all this stuff seems unnecessary.

True   *False*

| Always True | Often True | I Wish True | No Opinion | Often False | Always False |

My parents seem a bit concerned, so I am motivated to explore majors.

True   *False*

| Always True | Often True | I Wish True | No Opinion | Often False | Always False |

My parents seem extremely concerned, and that increases my anxiety about choosing a major.

True   *False*

| Always True | Often True | I Wish True | No Opinion | Often False | Always False |

I have financial issues that influence my choice of major.

True   *False*

| Always True | Often True | I Wish True | No Opinion | Often False | Always False |

I have gender issues associated with choosing a major.

True   *False*

| Always True | Often True | I Wish True | No Opinion | Often False | Always False |

I have cultural issues associated with choosing a major.

True   *False*

| Always True | Often True | I Wish True | No Opinion | Often False | Always False |

My inability to choose a major is negatively impacting my life.

True   *False*

| Always True | Often True | I Wish True | No Opinion | Often False | Always False |

Major Next Steps

I am very confused, unfocused, and need help.

True   *False*

| Always True | Often True | I Wish True | No Opinion | Often False | Always False |

I have too many major options in mind, so I want to narrow my list to three.

True   *False*

| Always True | Often True | I Wish True | No Opinion | Often False | Always False |

I am focused regarding majors, but need to identify and prioritize career options.

True   *False*

| Always True | Often True | I Wish True | No Opinion | Often False | Always False |

I am ready to declare a major.

True   *False*

| Always True | Often True | I Wish True | No Opinion | Often False | Always False |

I am just beginning to explore career options related to my major.

True   *False*

| Always True | Often True | I Wish True | No Opinion | Often False | Always False |

I can articulate and prioritize three career options related to my major.

True   *False*

| Always True | Often True | I Wish True | No Opinion | Often False | Always False |

I am ready to conduct a values assessment.

True   *False*

| Always True | Often True | I Wish True | No Opinion | Often False | Always False |

Now that you've read all of the test statements and answered each with a true or false, gauge your response for each one on the true-false continuum. You will inventory and examine your responses when you're done.

Remember from Chapter 1 that majors are best thought of as focused collections of academic experiences; they do not predict your future success. The relationships between majors and careers are important to identify and explore, but they shouldn't limit or frustrate you. Always keep in mind that second majors, minors, clusters, or one or two special courses can supplement any major you may choose.

Focus

Some high school and college students have a strong sense of academic and career focus. They are emotionally and intellectually ready to declare a major and confidently able to describe their related career goals. In order to choose a major, many of them just need to do some research, explore their options, and match the information they find to what they already know about themselves. Other students may be more confused and a bit anxious. For them, some structured activities and easily accessible information will provide the assurance they need to move forward. Your answers to the true-false questions in this test will reveal how ready you are. Completion of each test in this book is a positive step on your path to self-awareness, confidence, and a major decision. Your sense of accomplishment and achievement will grow test by test.

If you marked "always true" or "often true" to the statements about confusion and anxiety associated with majors or careers, rest assured that as you work through each chapter your anxiety should diminish. The more you understand about yourself and your interests, various majors, and the relationships between majors and possible careers, the more confident you'll become.

Your attitude can affect the outcome of the whole process of selecting a major. It's a bit of an oversimplification, but decisions about majors are best made with your intellect rather than your emotions. Your sense of focus will strengthen as you complete the assessment and research activities in this and subsequent chapters.

Academic Interests

Sometimes just writing down what interests you academically is all you need to focus on a major. But just being interested in a subject isn't enough to base your entire academic career on it. You must follow up by actively learning more in order to turn that initial gut reaction into a well-thought-out decision.

Look through the interests that you are always or often curious about. Now compare those to your list of first-glance majors:

- Do any majors show up on both the test and the list?
- Even if there are no majors in common, how many total options have you identified as worthy of further research?
- How strongly do you feel about the ones you've marked?
- Which of your academic interests are the strongest?
- Which ones do you want to begin researching immediately?

Career Interests

Now compare the careers that you marked as ones you are always or often curious about to the careers linked to your first-glance majors:

- Do you see any overlap?
- Which careers interest you most strongly?
- Which ones do you want to begin to research immediately?
- Are these careers interesting enough to you to encourage you to focus on a particular major, or at least on the courses you'll take next?
- Can you estimate the amount of assessment or research you need to do in order to feel comfortable linking a major to careers and then committing to that major?

Assessment and Research

Assessment and research might seem like too much work or a waste of time, but they make up two-thirds of the strategy that will ARM you for success. Done honestly and thoroughly, assessment and research will help you make a decision—not just an expedient decision made out of frustration, but a good decision that will help your future academic success. You aren't alone in this process; there are many resources and people that can help you.

Perhaps you've already completed some formal or informal tests, including those that use codes to evaluate your interests and abilities, and they've been helpful. You are already a step ahead. Later chapters will show you how to use those three- or four-letter codes to guide your research. If you took some tests but didn't feel they were helpful, don't worry. Later exercises in this book will help you understand your values, interests, personality traits, and skills and will sufficiently ARM you to make decisions about your major.

It's important that you know where to find and how to use the resources that will support you in your research. If you marked "no opinion," "often false," or "always false" to the statements associated with research resources, please refer to Appendix B. There you'll find a list of print and online resources that will get you started. Also, discuss your circumstances, thoughts, and concerns with academic advisors, instructors, and career counselors. High schools and colleges offer advising and counseling services, with professionals available to inspire confidence and provide practical help with research efforts.

Making Decisions

How and when you make your decisions about your major will be determined by deadlines, your motivation, and the availability of resources. As you complete the exercises in this book, you will get closer to being able to declare a major and articulate career goals related to that major. Once you have completed the steps required to identify and prioritize your options, you will be ready to make some tentative decisions. Declare a major knowing that you can continue your research and change your mind—and your major—whenever you wish.

If you marked "always true" or "often true" to statements about concerns, try not to procrastinate or avoid making decisions because of your anxiety. The simple, incremental steps you make as you progress through the chapters of this book will eventually lead you to a clear picture of your goals. You have begun your assessment with the tests and exercises that you have already taken. Further research will help you connect your increased self-knowledge with information about majors and careers.

Seek the advice and counsel of others, particularly objective individuals who might include teachers, advisors, and career counselors. Visit your school's advising center and career center. Speak with professionals about the pressures you feel, and take their views into account. Often, a discussion can diminish your concerns and reveal options that you might have overlooked. And don't forget that major decisions are not irreversible. You can declare a major and then change your mind with little, if any, consequence. Review the results of the first three tests in this book. You may be closer to decisions than you think.

Influences

Particularly if they're supporting you financially, parents often have strong opinions about any decisions regarding your major or career. Well-meaning parents find it difficult to hear the response "I don't know" when they ask questions about your future. Let them know how you're progressing. Tell them about the self-knowledge you've gained by completing the exercises in this book, and describe how you plan to conduct your research. Remind them that minors, clusters, and additional courses can complement any major and enhance your potential for finding employment. They might be interested to hear about the information you find. Allay their fears by proving that you are taking logical steps toward making a decision, and they will probably ease the pressure on you.

Once you begin to take the steps needed to make decisions about your major and career, you should feel more empowered and in control. View these decisions as positive—not negative—influences on your life. They are simply crossroads on your path to success, places where you can pause and choose the direction you want to take to get to your next destination. A positive attitude will yield a positive outcome. The assessments and research resources outlined in this book will help put you in control.

Next Steps

It's important to know where you are on the ARM continuum of assessing, researching, and making a decision about declaring a major. If you're confused and need help, turn to the next chapter and continue your assessment. Soon, a better knowledge of your values, interests, personality traits, and skills will prepare you for your research. If you feel you're ready to begin research into specific majors, follow the guidelines summarized in the following sections and chapters. Even if you think you're ready to declare a major now, it can't hurt to pause and complete the tests and exercises in the next few chapters. You might make some interesting discoveries that you didn't know before.

Printed Resources

When starting your research you should check out the *Career Opportunities For . . .* series (Checkmark Books of Facts on File), the *Careers in . . .* series (VGM Career Books), and the *Great Jobs* series (VGM Career Books). Each of these publications offers significant information connecting majors and careers. They cover the most popular majors, including but not limited to English, business, political science, communication, psychology, foreign languages, accounting, biology, and liberal arts. These publications define an amazing array of opportunities within industries such as banking, finance, and insurance; advertising and public relations; film, music, and art; health care; sports; politics, government, and activism; law; fashion; television and radio; and publishing.

Web Resources

Type the phrase "What can I do with a major in _____" into a search engine, and you'll get something like 250 million hits. The phrase "major and careers" yields over 8 million hits. Resources are plentiful, but in most cases, the most popular results of your search (those at the top of the list) may be enough to help you in your major and career research. Two of the most interesting sites are the Collegeboard.com majors-and-careers site and the career services section of the Rutgers University Web site.

Collegeboard.com

The portion of this site called "Majors and Careers Central" (at *www.collegeboard.com*) identifies schools that might match a student's specific needs. It is among the most commonly used Web resources for secondary students as well as college freshmen and sophomores. A visit to the site uncovers the information you need to make major decisions and identify the schools that offer majors related to your abilities and interests.

Career Services at Rutgers

On the Rutgers's Web site, the College Majors and Career Information area (at *www.careerservices.rutgers.edu*) addresses career options for many majors. It also presents profiles and summaries of majors and related occupations, typical employers, and examples of jobs obtained by Rutgers graduates.

Person-to-Person Approaches

Talk to as many people as you can. Friends, family members, alumni of colleges and universities that interest you, people who majored in subjects of interest, and people in jobs that you are curious about are all good candidates for your research. You'll find a list of sample questions to get you started in Chapter 3. You'll think of others as you go along.

The term "networking" is often cited, yet not many students truly understand what it means. Simply defined, networking means seeking the assistance of others to achieve your goals. Employment networking involves seeking consideration, referrals, or advice about your efforts to find internships or a job. Career-exploration networking involves identifying career role models who can give you information about a field you're interested in—especially interesting here are the academic and career paths they took to reach their professional goals. Major networking involves seeking information from students in different majors to learn about required courses and the academic environment of different departments. People-to-people efforts can be fun and, frankly, the most informative and inspirational form of research. With time, people you meet as you network may become mentors and active advocates, supporting you as you proceed down your own path to success.

Chapter 5

Match Your Major to Your Values

To paraphrase Rabbi Jonathan Sacks, "Values are the songs we play on the MP3 player of the mind: any tune we choose so long as it does not disturb others." Your values, ethics, beliefs, and ideals are highly personal guiding principles that define you as an individual and influence everything you do, from interacting with others to finding the kind of work you like to do. Understanding your values will help you decide on a major that is rewarding, intellectually stimulating, and even fun.

5

Test Your Values

What values are most important to the way you conduct your life? Do they include compassion, creativity, integrity, spirituality, courage, or independence? What values guide your behavior in society? Are they altruism, fairness, eco-consciousness, or reliability? What about the values that are important to you in your work environment? Do they include autonomy, loyalty, generosity, dedication, or competitiveness? These and many other values are examples of the convictions that you believe are desirable and important in your life.

You may never have stopped to think about it before, but clarifying your values—reflecting on what is most important to you—can be a worthwhile exercise in self-discovery. Besides writing down what comes to mind, you might also search for published lists of values. You may find some that you want to add to your own list!

Values can be viewed and defined from the perspective of academics or careers. Some individuals clearly value artistic and aesthetic courses and careers. Others value problem-solving skills that use quantitative tools, techniques, and industry. Many value the process of studying and, in time, applying entrepreneurial and business concepts to academic and real-life contexts. While some value the examination of physical and theoretical scientific principles, others value the exploration of human thought, individual emotions and behaviors, and the undertakings of societies and cultures. Rating and ranking over forty values allows you to identify your motives for completing a particular major or seeking entry to a particular career field. Remember, these should be your own values, not those of your parents or others.

As you review each of the values statements appearing in the following exercise, envision yourself making these statements. Think about how strongly you relate to each statement and whether your feelings are academically oriented, career oriented, or both. You might value studying advertising, broadcast journalism, public relations, and communication. If so, it will help you to determine how strong these feelings are and how much you value the careers that are associated with these studies.

This true-false test encourages you to think about and rank some values commonly associated with various majors and careers. As you work through the test, mark your responses quickly. Don't try to stop and analyze each choice. Your gut reactions will give you a good idea of what you really feel.

Understanding your values will not only enhance your self-awareness, it will also help you prioritize tasks in college or in a job. You can use this knowledge of what's most important to you to guide your decisions about a major, a job, or any other life choice. Value-guided decisions will help you stay motivated and increase the likelihood that you will be satisfied with your choices.

Some of the statements on this test deal with intrinsic values, those associated with the essential nature of a subject or work, such as a major that affords you independence or lets you develop your creativity. Extrinsic values are those that relate to external conditions, such as the physical setting in which you live or work, the recognition you gain from your work, or your earning potential. For most people, a feeling of fulfillment in school or work results from a combination of intrinsic and extrinsic value judgments.

One point to remember is that your values will probably change as your life experience expands. You might find it valuable to take this test again later in your college career or work life.

True-False Test of Values

Aesthetics and Art Appreciation

I value the creative process of exploring, studying, appreciating, and sharing beauty of ideas or things.

True   *False*

Always True	Often True	I Wish True	No Opinion	Often False	Always False

Adventure, Thrills, and Excitement

I value the experience of frequent risk taking as well as physical challenges.

True   *False*

Always True	Often True	I Wish True	No Opinion	Often False	Always False

Altruism and Helping Others

I value the experience of doing something that enhances the circumstances of others, bettering individuals, and helping the community.

True   *False*

Always True	Often True	I Wish True	No Opinion	Often False	Always False

Artistic Creativity

I value completing creative tasks using various artistic media,
including but not limited to painting, sketching, sculpture, and carving.

True   *False*

| Always True | Often True | I Wish True | No Opinion | Often False | Always False |

Agricultural Topics and Issues

I value the study of agribusiness, agronomy, animal or food science, and related courses and concepts.

True   *False*

| Always True | Often True | I Wish True | No Opinion | Often False | Always False |

Architecture or Planning Topics and Issues

I value the study of architecture, planning, design, or related courses and concepts.

True   *False*

| Always True | Often True | I Wish True | No Opinion | Often False | Always False |

Area Studies Topics and Issues

I value the study of courses and concepts related to African, Asian, European,
Latin, Near-Eastern, or other specific geopolitical areas and cultures.

True   *False*

| Always True | Often True | I Wish True | No Opinion | Often False | Always False |

Biological or Biomedical Topics and Issues

I valued the study of courses and concepts related to biology, biochemistry, biotechnology, environmental issues, toxicology, and zoology.

True   *False*

| Always True | Often True | I Wish True | No Opinion | Often False | Always False |

Business Topics and Issues

I value the study of courses and concepts related to accounting, actuarial science, finance,
economics, human resources, marketing, or management information systems.

True   *False*

| Always True | Often True | I Wish True | No Opinion | Often False | Always False |

Communication and Journalism Topics and Issues

I value the study of courses and concepts related to advertising, broadcast journalism, public relations, and communications.

True   *False*

| Always True | Often True | I Wish True | No Opinion | Often False | Always False |

Completing Challenging Problems

I value the processes of completing complex and diverse questions and problems, of troubleshooting, and of problem solving.

True   *False*

| Always True | Often True | I Wish True | No Opinion | Often False | Always False |

Computer Science and Information Technology Topics and Issues

I value the study of courses and concepts related to computer science, information systems, networking, and Web design.

True   *False*

| Always True | Often True | I Wish True | No Opinion | Often False | Always False |

Creativity of Idea Generation

I value the process of generating new and innovative ideas, programs, policies, products, services, or procedures.

True   *False*

| Always True | Often True | I Wish True | No Opinion | Often False | Always False |

Creativity of Written Expression

I value the process of drafting, editing, and finalizing innovative and original documents, correspondence, or promotional materials.

True   *False*

| Always True | Often True | I Wish True | No Opinion | Often False | Always False |

Ecology and Environmental Issues

I value the process of completing projects or efforts that have a positive impact on nature and the environment.

True   *False*

| Always True | Often True | I Wish True | No Opinion | Often False | Always False |

Education Topics and Issues

I value the process of studying courses and concepts related to
counseling, curriculum and instruction, teaching, and special education.

True   *False*

| Always True | Often True | I Wish True | No Opinion | Often False | Always False |

Engineering Topics and Issues

I value the study of courses and concepts related to engineering in the following industries:
aerospace, biomedicine, ceramic, chemical, civil, computer, electrical, and/or manufacturing.

True   *False*

| Always True | Often True | I Wish True | No Opinion | Often False | Always False |

English Literature and Language Topics and Issues

I value the study of courses and concepts related to American literature,
British literature, comparative literature, and creative writing.

True   *False*

| Always True | Often True | I Wish True | No Opinion | Often False | Always False |

Ethnic, Cultural, and Gender-Studies Topics and Issues

I value the study of courses and concepts related to issues concerning African-American,
Asian-American, gender, Latino, Native-American, and/or women's ethnic and cultural issues.

True   *False*

| Always True | Often True | I Wish True | No Opinion | Often False | Always False |

Family, Food, Consumer, and Nutritional Sciences Topics and Issues

I value the study of courses and concepts related to child development,
consumer behavior, family and community services, and food science.

True   *False*

| Always True | Often True | I Wish True | No Opinion | Often False | Always False |

Fine Arts Topics and Issues

I value the study of art history, studio arts, graphic arts, sculpture, or related courses and concepts.

True   *False*

| Always True | Often True | I Wish True | No Opinion | Often False | Always False |

Group Interactions and Team Projects

I value the process of interacting with a group in order to achieve a common goal or complete projects.

True   *False*

| Always True | Often True | I Wish True | No Opinion | Often False | Always False |

Health Service and Allied Health-Care Topics and Issues

I value the study of courses and concepts related to athletic training,
audiology, dietetics, dental hygiene, and laboratory technology.

True   *False*

| Always True | Often True | I Wish True | No Opinion | Often False | Always False |

History Topics and Issues

I value the study of courses and concepts related to British, contemporary, European, and medieval history.

True   *False*

| Always True | Often True | I Wish True | No Opinion | Often False | Always False |

Independence

I value the experience of focusing on tasks, projects, and
processes without significant direction of supervisors.

True   *False*

| Always True | Often True | I Wish True | No Opinion | Often False | Always False |

Language, Literature, and Linguistics Topics and Issues

I value the study of courses and concepts related to Ancient Greek, Arabic, Chinese, French,
German, Hebrew, Italian, Japanese, and/or Modern Greek language and literature.

True   *False*

| Always True | Often True | I Wish True | No Opinion | Often False | Always False |

Law and Legal Studies Topics and Issues

I value the study of courses and concepts related to criminal
justice, legal studies, and paralegal and prelaw curricula.

True   *False*

| Always True | Often True | I Wish True | No Opinion | Often False | Always False |

Library Science Topics and Issues

I value the study of courses and concepts related to information science, library science, and library technology.

True   *False*

| Always True | Often True | I Wish True | No Opinion | Often False | Always False |

Mathematics and Statistics Topics and Issues

I value the study of courses and concepts related to actuarial science, applied mathematics, and statistics.

True   *False*

| Always True | Often True | I Wish True | No Opinion | Often False | Always False |

Mental, Social, and Public Health Topics and Issues

I value the study of courses and concepts related to addiction counseling, environmental health, occupational health, and public health.

True   *False*

| Always True | Often True | I Wish True | No Opinion | Often False | Always False |

Multidisciplinary and Interdisciplinary Studies Topics and Issues

I value the study of courses and concepts related to ancient studies, behavioral sciences, biochemistry, and health and society.

True   *False*

| Always True | Often True | I Wish True | No Opinion | Often False | Always False |

Natural Resources and Conservation Topics and Issues

I value the study of courses and concepts related to ecology, environmental sciences, forestry, and natural resources.

True   *False*

| Always True | Often True | I Wish True | No Opinion | Often False | Always False |

Parks, Recreation, and Fitness Topics and Issues

I value the study of courses and concepts related to exercise science, health and physical fitness, and sports management.

True   *False*

| Always True | Often True | I Wish True | No Opinion | Often False | Always False |

Performing Arts Topics and Issues

I value the study of acting, dance, theatre, film studies, music, or related courses and concepts.

True   *False*

| Always True | Often True | I Wish True | No Opinion | Often False | Always False |

Philosophy Topics and Issues

I value the study of argumentation, ethics, and philosophy.

True   *False*

| Always True | Often True | I Wish True | No Opinion | Often False | Always False |

Physical Demands

I value the opportunity to use physical strength, speed, and/or agility to complete tasks.

True   *False*

| Always True | Often True | I Wish True | No Opinion | Often False | Always False |

Physical Sciences Topics and Issues

I value the study of courses and concepts related to astronomy, chemistry, meteorology, and physics.

True   *False*

| Always True | Often True | I Wish True | No Opinion | Often False | Always False |

Psychology Topics and Issues

I value the study of adolescent, behavioral, clinical, educational, and
social psychology and related courses and concepts.

True   *False*

| Always True | Often True | I Wish True | No Opinion | Often False | Always False |

Public Administration and Social Services Topics and Issues

I value the study of advocacy, health and human services, public administration and public policy, and related courses and concepts.

True   *False*

| Always True | Often True | I Wish True | No Opinion | Often False | Always False |

Quantitative Research, Analysis, and Problem Solving

I value the process of completing data and analytical tasks and presenting potential outcomes and solutions.

True   *False*

| Always True | Often True | I Wish True | No Opinion | Often False | Always False |

Religious Studies and Theology Studies Topics and Issues

I value the study of religion, pastoral counseling, rabbinical, and theology and related courses and concepts.

True   *False*

| Always True | Often True | I Wish True | No Opinion | Often False | Always False |

Security, Protective Services, and Justice Topics and Issues

I value the study of corrections, criminal justice, law enforcement, police science, and related courses and concepts.

True   *False*

| Always True | Often True | I Wish True | No Opinion | Often False | Always False |

Social Science Topics and Issues

I value the study of courses and concepts related to anthropology,
economics, archeology, geography, sociology, and urban studies.

True   *False*

| Always True | Often True | I Wish True | No Opinion | Often False | Always False |

Therapy and Rehabilitation Topics and Issues

I value the study of courses and concepts related to art, music, occupational, and physical therapy.

True   *False*

| Always True | Often True | I Wish True | No Opinion | Often False | Always False |

Look at your responses to the values test and follow these steps:

1. Use highlighters or pens of different colors to categorize your different responses (such as blue for "always true," yellow for "often true," and so on).
2. Identify those values you marked as "I wish true"?
3. Think about why you wish you had these values. Make notes in the margins.
4. Determine which were your top ten values, and list those on the College Major Values Grid (page 93).

Majors and Values

Yes, your values are important. But how does knowing your values influence your choice of a major? To analyze your results, you need to complete the Values Grid. Refer to the information in Chapter 2, the appendices, and at the end of this chapter to help you fill out the sections that ask you to identify potential majors and courses associated with different values. The research you do will be key here and help you later. But identifying your values is just the beginning. In the next chapter you'll assess your interests.

College Major Values Grid

Values Statements Ranked in Order of Significance	How Values Could Be Incorporated	Potential Courses and Majors
"Always true" and "often true" values that must be incorporated into decisions, listed in order of significance.	Ways each statement can be applied to an academic context.	Courses and majors you believe are associated with each statement (using Chapter 2 and appendices for reference, if necessary).
1.		
2.		
3.		
4.		
5.		
6.		
7.		
8.		
9.		
10.		

The five most significant values that motivate my exploration of majors:

1.
2.
3.
4.
5.

Now address those statements identified as "I wish true."

Wish-Were-True Values Statements in Order of Significance	How Values Could Be Enhanced or Internalized	Potential Courses and Majors
"I wish true" values statements, ranked in order of significance.	Ways you can nurture each value.	Courses and majors you believe are associated with each statement.
1.		
2.		
3.		
4.		
5.		
The three most significant values that I wish to enhance:		
1.		
2.		
3.		
Describe why you wish these values statements were true:		

Using a new approach, reveal new perspectives by completing the exercise below.

Major Interests	Values Connected to Interests
List majors you are curious about or are currently actively exploring.	Review the True-False Values Test. For each major you list, identify three values statements you associate most closely with that major.
1.	1. 2. 3.
2.	1. 2. 3.
3.	1. 2. 3.
4.	1. 2. 3.
5.	1. 2. 3.
Three most significant "always true" or "often true" values that are associated with your career interests:	
1. 2. 3.	

For those of you who would like more information about values, here are a couple of helpful Web sites that offer other assessment exercises, standardized tests, and resources:

- *www.careerkey.org.* This site contains links and assessments that measure values, interests, personality, and skills.
- *www.testingroom.com.* This site features self-assessment of values, personality traits, and more, and links to other online tests. Offers short reports for free and more detailed reports for a fee.

While the informal true-false tests you have already completed can yield meaningful and powerful results, it would also be interesting to compare results of these activities to more formal tests like those offered in these two sites.

Chapter 6

Match Your Major to Your Interests

Dag Hammarskjöld, former Secretary General of the United Nations, once said, "We are not permitted to choose the frame of our destiny, but what we put into it is ours." Your destiny has not yet been determined, but the components of you are already well established and will play a large role in framing your future. In this chapter, you will assess your interests and find out how they relate to your possible college major options.

Test Your Interests

This test is designed to identify those subjects and activities that interest you the most. Once again, you'll review and prioritize the results of this test and add those results to what you learned from the values test. Don't fret over the questions—just mark your first reaction to each item. All of this information will help you decide on a major in a field of study that interests you.

As you review this list of majors, job titles, and career fields, your initial impressions will reveal the strength of your interest in each. First impressions are what you wish to document. Don't dwell too long on any one statement.

If you identify a particular major, job, or field that you don't know enough about to judge, circle the statement rather than answering the question. Then do some quick research to enhance your knowledge and determine the strength of your interests.

The patterns revealed upon completion of this true-false test will be most important. They may reinforce information you have already identified through the first-glance majors exercise, the values test, or other assessments. Alternately, your answers to this test may inspire additional research. Once you have rated and ranked your interests and then compared them with results of previous assessments, you will be closer to identifying and prioritizing majors worthy of research and those you might choose as your own.

True-False Test of Interests
When thinking of majors, I am interested in:

Accounting

True   *False*

Always True	Often True	I Wish True	Often False	Always False

Actuarial sciences

True   *False*

Always True	Often True	I Wish True	Often False	Always False

Advertising

True   *False*

Always True	Often True	I Wish True	Often False	Always False

Advising

True   *False*

Always True   Often True   I Wish True   Often False   Always False

Agriculture

True   *False*

Always True   Often True   I Wish True   Often False   Always False

Allied health care

True   *False*

Always True   Often True   I Wish True   Often False   Always False

American history

True   *False*

Always True   Often True   I Wish True   Often False   Always False

American literature

True   *False*

Always True   Often True   I Wish True   Often False   Always False

Anthropology

True   *False*

Always True   Often True   I Wish True   Often False   Always False

Archeology

True   *False*

Always True   Often True   I Wish True   Often False   Always False

Architecture and planning

True   *False*

Always True   Often True   I Wish True   Often False   Always False

Art

True   *False*

Always True   Often True   I Wish True   Often False   Always False

Art therapy

True   *False*

| Always True | Often True | I Wish True | Often False | Always False |

Astronomy

True   *False*

| Always True | Often True | I Wish True | Often False | Always False |

Astrophysics

True   *False*

| Always True | Often True | I Wish True | Often False | Always False |

Athletics

True   *False*

| Always True | Often True | I Wish True | Often False | Always False |

Athletic training

True   *False*

| Always True | Often True | I Wish True | Often False | Always False |

Adolescent psychology

True   *False*

| Always True | Often True | I Wish True | Often False | Always False |

Audiology and speech pathology

True   *False*

| Always True | Often True | I Wish True | Often False | Always False |

Banking

True   *False*

| Always True | Often True | I Wish True | Often False | Always False |

Behavioral psychology

True   *False*

| Always True | Often True | I Wish True | Often False | Always False |

Bilingual education

True   *False*

Always True   Often True   I Wish True   Often False   Always False

Biological or biomedical science

True   *False*

Always True   Often True   I Wish True   Often False   Always False

Biomedical engineering

True   *False*

Always True   Often True   I Wish True   Often False   Always False

Biotechnology

True   *False*

Always True   Often True   I Wish True   Often False   Always False

British literature

True   *False*

Always True   Often True   I Wish True   Often False   Always False

Broadcast media

True   *False*

Always True   Often True   I Wish True   Often False   Always False

Building

True   *False*

Always True   Often True   I Wish True   Often False   Always False

Business

True   *False*

Always True   Often True   I Wish True   Often False   Always False

Carpentry or woodworking

True   *False*

Always True   Often True   I Wish True   Often False   Always False

Chemical engineering

True   *False*

| Always True | Often True | I Wish True | Often False | Always False |

Chemistry

True   *False*

| Always True | Often True | I Wish True | Often False | Always False |

Child care

True   *False*

| Always True | Often True | I Wish True | Often False | Always False |

Child development

True   *False*

| Always True | Often True | I Wish True | Often False | Always False |

City or regional planning

True   *False*

| Always True | Often True | I Wish True | Often False | Always False |

Civil engineering

True   *False*

| Always True | Often True | I Wish True | Often False | Always False |

Communication and journalism

True   *False*

| Always True | Often True | I Wish True | Often False | Always False |

Computer engineering

True   *False*

| Always True | Often True | I Wish True | Often False | Always False |

Computer programming

True   *False*

| Always True | Often True | I Wish True | Often False | Always False |

Computer science

True   *False*

Always True	Often True	I Wish True	Often False	Always False

Conservation

True   *False*

Always True	Often True	I Wish True	Often False	Always False

Consumer behavior

True   *False*

Always True	Often True	I Wish True	Often False	Always False

Coaching

True   *False*

Always True	Often True	I Wish True	Often False	Always False

Counseling

True   *False*

Always True	Often True	I Wish True	Often False	Always False

Creative writing

True   *False*

Always True	Often True	I Wish True	Often False	Always False

Criminology

True   *False*

Always True	Often True	I Wish True	Often False	Always False

Criminal justice

True   *False*

Always True	Often True	I Wish True	Often False	Always False

Culinary arts

True   *False*

Always True	Often True	I Wish True	Often False	Always False

Data management

True   *False*

Always True	Often True	I Wish True	Often False	Always False

Debate and forensics

True   *False*

Always True	Often True	I Wish True	Often False	Always False

Dietetics

True   *False*

Always True	Often True	I Wish True	Often False	Always False

Dentistry

True   *False*

Always True	Often True	I Wish True	Often False	Always False

Dental hygiene

True   *False*

Always True	Often True	I Wish True	Often False	Always False

Developmental psychology

True   *False*

Always True	Often True	I Wish True	Often False	Always False

Drama

True   *False*

Always True	Often True	I Wish True	Often False	Always False

Economics

True   *False*

Always True	Often True	I Wish True	Often False	Always False

E-commerce

True   *False*

Always True	Often True	I Wish True	Often False	Always False

Education

True   *False*

| Always True | Often True | I Wish True | Often False | Always False |

Electrical engineering

True   *False*

| Always True | Often True | I Wish True | Often False | Always False |

Elementary education

True   *False*

| Always True | Often True | I Wish True | Often False | Always False |

Engineering

True   *False*

| Always True | Often True | I Wish True | Often False | Always False |

English language and literature

True   *False*

| Always True | Often True | I Wish True | Often False | Always False |

Entrepreneurship

True   *False*

| Always True | Often True | I Wish True | Often False | Always False |

Environmental engineering

True   *False*

| Always True | Often True | I Wish True | Often False | Always False |

Environmental studies

True   *False*

| Always True | Often True | I Wish True | Often False | Always False |

Ethics

True   *False*

| Always True | Often True | I Wish True | Often False | Always False |

Ethnic, cultural, and gender studies

True   *False*

| Always True | Often True | I Wish True | Often False | Always False |

European history

True   *False*

| Always True | Often True | I Wish True | Often False | Always False |

Event planning

True   *False*

| Always True | Often True | I Wish True | Often False | Always False |

Exercise science

True   *False*

| Always True | Often True | I Wish True | Often False | Always False |

Experimental psychology

True   *False*

| Always True | Often True | I Wish True | Often False | Always False |

Family and community service

True   *False*

| Always True | Often True | I Wish True | Often False | Always False |

Film and video production

True   *False*

| Always True | Often True | I Wish True | Often False | Always False |

Food and nutrition

True   *False*

| Always True | Often True | I Wish True | Often False | Always False |

Foreign languages

True   *False*

| Always True | Often True | I Wish True | Often False | Always False |

Forestry

True   *False*

| Always True | Often True | I Wish True | Often False | Always False |

Fundraising

True   *False*

| Always True | Often True | I Wish True | Often False | Always False |

Government

True   *False*

| Always True | Often True | I Wish True | Often False | Always False |

Graphic Arts

True   *False*

| Always True | Often True | I Wish True | Often False | Always False |

Health care administration

True   *False*

| Always True | Often True | I Wish True | Often False | Always False |

Health and human services

True   *False*

| Always True | Often True | I Wish True | Often False | Always False |

Health and wellness

True   *False*

| Always True | Often True | I Wish True | Often False | Always False |

Higher education teaching or administration

True   *False*

| Always True | Often True | I Wish True | Often False | Always False |

History

True   *False*

| Always True | Often True | I Wish True | Often False | Always False |

Hotel or resort management

True   *False*

Always True	Often True	I Wish True	Often False	Always False

Human resources

True   *False*

Always True	Often True	I Wish True	Often False	Always False

Human services

True   *False*

Always True	Often True	I Wish True	Often False	Always False

Information systems

True   *False*

Always True	Often True	I Wish True	Often False	Always False

Insurance

True   *False*

Always True	Often True	I Wish True	Often False	Always False

International relations

True   *False*

Always True	Often True	I Wish True	Often False	Always False

Investments

True   *False*

Always True	Often True	I Wish True	Often False	Always False

Labor and industrial relations

True   *False*

Always True	Often True	I Wish True	Often False	Always False

Laboratory research

True   *False*

Always True	Often True	I Wish True	Often False	Always False

Laboratory science

True   *False*

| Always True | Often True | I Wish True | Often False | Always False |

Law

True   *False*

| Always True | Often True | I Wish True | Often False | Always False |

Law enforcement

True   *False*

| Always True | Often True | I Wish True | Often False | Always False |

Library science

True   *False*

| Always True | Often True | I Wish True | Often False | Always False |

Linguistics

True   *False*

| Always True | Often True | I Wish True | Often False | Always False |

Literature

True   *False*

| Always True | Often True | I Wish True | Often False | Always False |

Lobbying

True   *False*

| Always True | Often True | I Wish True | Often False | Always False |

Marketing

True   *False*

| Always True | Often True | I Wish True | Often False | Always False |

Marketing research

True   *False*

| Always True | Often True | I Wish True | Often False | Always False |

Mathematics

True   *False*

| Always True | Often True | I Wish True | Often False | Always False |

Mortgage banking and real estate finance

True   *False*

| Always True | Often True | I Wish True | Often False | Always False |

Management

True   *False*

| Always True | Often True | I Wish True | Often False | Always False |

Management information systems

True   *False*

| Always True | Often True | I Wish True | Often False | Always False |

Material science

True   *False*

| Always True | Often True | I Wish True | Often False | Always False |

Mechanical activities

True   *False*

| Always True | Often True | I Wish True | Often False | Always False |

Mechanical engineering

True   *False*

| Always True | Often True | I Wish True | Often False | Always False |

Medical science

True   *False*

| Always True | Often True | I Wish True | Often False | Always False |

Mental health

True   *False*

| Always True | Often True | I Wish True | Often False | Always False |

Armed services

True   *False*

| Always True | Often True | I Wish True | Often False | Always False |

Mining and metallurgy

True   *False*

| Always True | Often True | I Wish True | Often False | Always False |

Music

True   *False*

| Always True | Often True | I Wish True | Often False | Always False |

Music therapy

True   *False*

| Always True | Often True | I Wish True | Often False | Always False |

Nature and the environment

True   *False*

| Always True | Often True | I Wish True | Often False | Always False |

Nuclear engineering

True   *False*

| Always True | Often True | I Wish True | Often False | Always False |

Nursing

True   *False*

| Always True | Often True | I Wish True | Often False | Always False |

Natural resources

True   *False*

| Always True | Often True | I Wish True | Often False | Always False |

Natural science

True   *False*

| Always True | Often True | I Wish True | Often False | Always False |

Nutrition

True   *False*

Always True   Often True   I Wish True   Often False   Always False

Occupational therapy

True   *False*

Always True   Often True   I Wish True   Often False   Always False

Oceanography

True   *False*

Always True   Often True   I Wish True   Often False   Always False

Office management

True   *False*

Always True   Often True   I Wish True   Often False   Always False

Organic chemistry

True   *False*

Always True   Often True   I Wish True   Often False   Always False

Organizational management

True   *False*

Always True   Often True   I Wish True   Often False   Always False

Organizational psychology

True   *False*

Always True   Often True   I Wish True   Often False   Always False

Paralegal

True   *False*

Always True   Often True   I Wish True   Often False   Always False

Patient care

True   *False*

Always True   Often True   I Wish True   Often False   Always False

Performing arts

True   *False*

| Always True | Often True | I Wish True | Often False | Always False |

Pharmaceutical science

True   *False*

| Always True | Often True | I Wish True | Often False | Always False |

Philosophy

True   *False*

| Always True | Often True | I Wish True | Often False | Always False |

Photography

True   *False*

| Always True | Often True | I Wish True | Often False | Always False |

Physical therapy

True   *False*

| Always True | Often True | I Wish True | Often False | Always False |

Physics

True   *False*

| Always True | Often True | I Wish True | Often False | Always False |

Physician

True   *False*

| Always True | Often True | I Wish True | Often False | Always False |

Physician's assistant

True   *False*

| Always True | Often True | I Wish True | Often False | Always False |

Physiology

True   *False*

| Always True | Often True | I Wish True | Often False | Always False |

Politics

True   *False*

Always True	Often True	I Wish True	Often False	Always False

Policy analysis

True   *False*

Always True	Often True	I Wish True	Often False	Always False

Preschool teaching or care

True   *False*

Always True	Often True	I Wish True	Often False	Always False

Print media

True   *False*

Always True	Often True	I Wish True	Often False	Always False

Psychiatry

True   *False*

Always True	Often True	I Wish True	Often False	Always False

Psychology

True   *False*

Always True	Often True	I Wish True	Often False	Always False

Psychological therapy

True   *False*

Always True	Often True	I Wish True	Often False	Always False

Psychology research

True   *False*

Always True	Often True	I Wish True	Often False	Always False

Public administration

True   *False*

Always True	Often True	I Wish True	Often False	Always False

Public policy

True   *False*

Always True   Often True   I Wish True   Often False   Always False

Public relations

True   *False*

Always True   Often True   I Wish True   Often False   Always False

Public safety and police services

True   *False*

Always True   Often True   I Wish True   Often False   Always False

Public service

True   *False*

Always True   Often True   I Wish True   Often False   Always False

Public speaking

True   *False*

Always True   Often True   I Wish True   Often False   Always False

Publishing

True   *False*

Always True   Often True   I Wish True   Often False   Always False

Recreation

True   *False*

Always True   Often True   I Wish True   Often False   Always False

Religious activities

True   *False*

Always True   Often True   I Wish True   Often False   Always False

Religious education

True   *False*

Always True   Often True   I Wish True   Often False   Always False

Religious studies

True   *False*

| Always True | Often True | I Wish True | Often False | Always False |

Robotics

True   *False*

| Always True | Often True | I Wish True | Often False | Always False |

Restaurant and food management

True   *False*

| Always True | Often True | I Wish True | Often False | Always False |

Sales

True   *False*

| Always True | Often True | I Wish True | Often False | Always False |

Scientific research

True   *False*

| Always True | Often True | I Wish True | Often False | Always False |

Secondary education

True   *False*

| Always True | Often True | I Wish True | Often False | Always False |

Social psychology

True   *False*

| Always True | Often True | I Wish True | Often False | Always False |

Social science research

True   *False*

| Always True | Often True | I Wish True | Often False | Always False |

Social services

True   *False*

| Always True | Often True | I Wish True | Often False | Always False |

Social work

True   *False*

| Always True | Often True | I Wish True | Often False | Always False |

Sociology

True   *False*

| Always True | Often True | I Wish True | Often False | Always False |

Special education

True   *False*

| Always True | Often True | I Wish True | Often False | Always False |

Speech and language therapy

True   *False*

| Always True | Often True | I Wish True | Often False | Always False |

Sport management and marketing

True   *False*

| Always True | Often True | I Wish True | Often False | Always False |

Statistics

True   *False*

| Always True | Often True | I Wish True | Often False | Always False |

Studio arts

True   *False*

| Always True | Often True | I Wish True | Often False | Always False |

Systems management

True   *False*

| Always True | Often True | I Wish True | Often False | Always False |

Teaching

True   *False*

| Always True | Often True | I Wish True | Often False | Always False |

Theatre

True   *False*

| Always True | Often True | I Wish True | Often False | Always False |

Theological studies

True   *False*

| Always True | Often True | I Wish True | Often False | Always False |

Urban and regional planning

True   *False*

| Always True | Often True | I Wish True | Often False | Always False |

Urban studies

True   *False*

| Always True | Often True | I Wish True | Often False | Always False |

Web design

True   *False*

| Always True | Often True | I Wish True | Often False | Always False |

Wildlife management

True   *False*

| Always True | Often True | I Wish True | Often False | Always False |

Writing

True   *False*

| Always True | Often True | I Wish True | Often False | Always False |

After you have completed the test, review your responses and answer the following questions:

- What interests did you identify as "always true" or "often true"?
- Which ones did you mark "I wish true"?
- Do you have any thoughts about why you might be interested in these areas?

Next, highlight your top ten interests. To summarize the results of this test, take a few minutes to complete the Interests Grid on page 124. After you complete this grid, compare it to the Values Grid and to your first-glance majors and answer the following questions:

- Are clear patterns now being revealed?
- Do certain majors, jobs, and career fields appear over and over?
- Are there entries that surprise you?

What's Your Holland Code?

Generations of students have completed innumerable tests that purported to tell them what they should do with their lives. Perhaps you've been introduced to various "interest inventories" before and have been assigned a two-, three-, or four-letter code or type. While no one can be completely summed up in one group of letters, an understanding of the concepts related to these codes can help you link your interests to potentially suitable majors and careers. We'll focus on two code systems in particular: the Strong Interest Inventory, created by E. K. Strong, Ph.D., and the Holland code, developed by John L. Holland, Ph.D.

The Strong Interest Inventory

In the 1920s, researcher E. K. Strong developed an assessment tool that would collect information about a person's preferences and inclinations for the purpose of placing military recruits in suitable jobs. Strong theorized that individuals who worked in occupations that they found interesting would feel fulfilled and satisfied in their jobs. In 1927, Strong and Stanford

University published the Strong Interest Inventory for use with the general public, and it is still the most commonly used interest test. Since its debut, the Strong Interest Inventory has been regularly revised, improved, and updated. The assessment now includes the addition of Dr. Holland's theories of basic personality types.

Holland Codes

In 1966, psychologist Dr. John Holland published *The Psychology of Vocational Choice,* in which he summarized his theory that people could be grouped into six basic types—realistic, investigative, artistic, social, enterprising, and conventional (RIASEC)—and that the same basic types could be used to describe work environments. People enjoy working in environments that let them use their abilities, feel satisfied, and avoid tasks they dislike. The match of worker to work environment determines how much a person enjoys his or her job. Dr. Holland published his first formal assessment, the Self-Directed Search, in 1971. Since then, many other formal and informal assessments have been developed that use his ideas.

Read the following table to determine which of the Holland codes applies to you. The table also allows you to estimate how you would be assessed according to Myers-Briggs (described in further detail on page 143).

Holland Codes, Myers-Briggs Codes, and Majors

Realistic (R)	*Investigative (I)*
People with athletic or mechanical ability; work well with machines, tools, animals, or plants. Prefer to work outdoors. Physically transform plans into results.	People who observe, learn, investigate, analyze, evaluate, and solve problems. Gravitate to scientific and technical fields.
Potential Fields, Functions, and Majors	**Potential Fields, Functions, and Majors**
Forestry, industrial arts, engineering, mechanical engineering, agriculture and mining, civil and industrial engineering, drafting, landscape architecture, technician, environmental science, veterinary medicine, geology, and arborist. Includes skilled trades, technicians, and engineers.	Economist, internist, physician, anthropology, astronomy, pathologist, physicist, chemist, lab assistant, medical assistant, biologist, osteopath, chiropractor, math and science teacher, researcher, analyst, pharmacist, actuary, computer science, geology, zoology, horticulture, natural science, oceanography, biochemistry, veterinary medicine, X-ray technology, aeronautics engineering, chemical engineering, electrical engineering, and computer science.
Skills and Competencies	**Skills and Competencies**
Drafting, reading plans and blueprints, repairing, using tools, making drawings and plans, using machines, as well as mathematical and mechanical aptitude.	Reading and understanding medical and scientific literature, working in laboratory, medical, or scientific settings, working on scientific projects, using scientific and medical equipment, solving mathematical problems, taking and excelling in science courses.
Related Myers-Briggs Code	**Related Myers-Briggs Code**
Sensing-Thinking	Intuitive-Thinking
Conventional (C)	*Artistic (A)*
People who work with data, using numerical, administrative, or related skills. Very detail-focused and able to follow instructions to complete diverse and multiple tasks.	People with artistic, musical, literary, and creative talents. Intuitive strength; like to work in unstructured settings, using creativity and imagination.
Potential Fields, Functions, and Majors	**Potential Fields, Functions, and Majors**
Accounting, business, information technology, and computer science. Administrative assistant, bookkeeper, and editorial or production assistant.	Drama, English, journalism, foreign languages, philosophy, art, literature, and music. Teacher, performer, advertising executive, entertainer, public relations professional, writer, editor, media broadcaster, actor, designer, and photographer.

Skills and Competencies	**Skills and Competencies**
Maintaining financial and other records, completing business tasks and transactions, and following instructions, focusing on details.	Painting, sketching, drawing, designing, and building; playing an instrument, writing, illustrating, and completing creative projects.
Related Myers-Briggs Code Sensing-Thinking	**Related Myers-Briggs Code** Intuitive-Thinking Intuitive-Feeling
Enterprising (E) People who influence others, sell, persuade, oversee business and entrepreneurial activities, give presentations, lead a group to achieve specific goals, and spearhead an enterprise.	***Social (S)*** People who explain things to and motivate others, plan activities and projects, and judge personalities and circumstances. Relationship-oriented strength with potential to help, enlighten, teach, or cure.
Potential Fields, Functions, and Majors Marketing, business, management, finance, real estate, government, political science, law, marketing analyst, banker, underwriter, appraiser, broadcast media professional, insurance agent, personnel professional, retail store owner and manager, lawyer, judge, political office holder.	**Potential Fields, Functions, and Majors** Sociology, psychology, education, counseling, religion, human services, counselor or advisor, public relations professional, recreation worker, nurse, political scientist, politician, legislative aide, college professor, social worker, librarian, history teacher, therapist, psychologist, trainer, and human resource professional.
Skills and Competencies Presenting political or policy views. Supervising and motivating others. Expressing energy, enthusiasm, and persuasive talents. Sales talents. Entrepreneurial spirit. Debate skills.	**Skills and Competencies** Explaining to others, motivating others to change or grow, teaching, training, planning, nurturing, and implementing events or discussions.
Related Myers-Briggs Code Sensing-Thinking Intuitive-Thinking	**Related Myers-Briggs Code** Intuitive-Feeling Sensing-Feeling

Dr. Holland's six occupational personality types have been used worldwide to help people make effective career choices; for instance, in 1972, Richard Bolles popularized the use of Holland personality types for the general public in his book, *What Color Is Your Parachute?* It can also be used to help you choose a major. Bear in mind that each personality type is a pure, or idealized, type, and that one person will rarely, if ever, personify one type. Your vocational personality will probably combine varying degrees of several types. Use of your Holland code is intended to inspire you to explore your options in majors and careers; it can't predict your future success or happiness. Nor will it tell you to enter any particular occupation, as some students mistakenly believe.

Consider your Holland code just one piece of your self-knowledge puzzle. Combined with the results of all of the assessments in this book and elsewhere, it will give you more data with which to guide your academic career.

Read through the descriptions of the Holland types contained in the previous pages and the table on page 126. Do you see any that seem to describe you? Often just selecting the three that resonate the most strongly with you can inspire you to research academic fields you may never have considered before. Once you have identified the code that you think best describes you and noted the related careers, list some potential majors associated with those careers. Ask yourself the following questions:

- What is your strongest type?
- What are your second strongest and third strongest types?
- What is your three-letter code?
- What majors, minors, or courses correspond with your strongest type and three-letter code?

RIASEC and a person's three-letter code are commonly found in the lexicon of career counselors. You won't be a Holland code expert, but you should be familiar with your own code, its uses, and how it can help you in your ARM strategy of assessment, research, and making a decision about your major. Look for some of the publications that list majors and careers using the Holland codes.

Interests and Majors

Now look at what you have learned from the true-false interests test (page 98) combined with an understanding of your Holland code. Complete the Interests Grid, including the lists of potential majors and courses associated with your significant interests (for help, refer to the appendices).

College Major Interests Grid

Fields of Interest Ranked in Order of Significance	Potential Courses, Majors, and Job Titles
"Always true" and "often true" interests that must be incorporated into decisions, listed in order of significance.	*Use Chapter 9 information, easily identifiable associations between true-false statements and majors, as well as a course catalog to identify courses, majors, and job titles you believe are associated with each field.*
1.	
2.	
3	
4.	
5.	
6.	
7.	
8.	
9	
10.	
Describe why you listed your top three interests above; identify majors associated with those fields:	
Note the Holland Code that you think best describes you and identify majors associated with this code:	

Now, let's address "I wish true" interests. Again, these may be significant results of your test.

Wish-True Interests in Order of Significance	How Interests Could Be Expanded Upon	Potential Courses, Majors, and Careers
"I wish true" interests statements ranked in order of significance.	*Ways you can nurture each interest.*	*Courses, majors, and careers you believe are associated with each interest.*
1.		
2.		
3		
4.		
5.		
The most significant interests that I wish to expand upon:		
Describe why you wish the above interests were true:		

Holland Codes, Values, Interests, and Skills	
Using this list of Web-based or other assessments, including the Self-Initiated Search or Strong Interest Inventory, identify your strongest Holland three-letter code.	
Realistic	**Values, Interests, and Skills**
	Values practicality and common sense. Interests include machines, tools, and the outdoors. Skills are related to operating equipment, using tools, and building and repairing, as well as mechanical ingenuity and dexterity and physical coordination.
Investigative	**Values, Interests, and Skills**
	Values independence, curiosity, and learning. Interests include science, theories, ideas, and data. Skills are related to performing lab work, solving abstract problems, and researching, as well as mathematics, writing, and analysis.
Artistic	**Values, Interests, and Skills**
	Values independence, beauty, originality, and imagination. Interests include self-expression, art appreciation, and the arts. Skills are related to creativity and musical and artistic expression, as well as composing music, writing, and creating visual art.
Social	**Values, Interests, and Skills**
	Values cooperation, service to others, altruism, and generosity. Interests in people, team work, human welfare, and community service. Skills are related to interaction with others, verbal abilities, listening, and understanding, as well as teaching, coaching, explaining, and helping.
Enterprising	**Values, Interests, and Skills**
	Values risk-taking, status, and competition. Interests include business, politics, leadership, and influence. Skills are related to verbal abilities; motivational talents; and overseeing activities; as well as selling, managing, persuading and inspiring.
Conventional	**Values, Interests, and Skills**
	Values accuracy, stability, and efficiency. Interests in organization, data, finance, and related matters. Skills related to math, data analysis, record keeping, and attention to detail, as well as setting-up procedures and organizing and operating computer and electrical equipment.

Review your selected answers and perform the following two steps:

1. List the careers and job functions associated with your strongest three-letter code.
2. List the three most significant careers and job functions associated with your strongest three-letter code.

Inventories and tests like the ones in this book reveal patterns of interests and connect them to a variety of majors and career fields. While you may discover that you are interested in a particular major or career, that fact doesn't tell you whether or not you have the aptitude (skills) or motivation (values and personality) to succeed in that field. Using all of the assessments and resources at your disposal, however, will focus your academic efforts and lessen the chances that you'll choose a major that is wrong for you or that you later find you dislike.

Regardless of whether you use a three-letter code or simply a list of the fields most interesting to you, you will be better able to focus your research and eventually choose a major. There are lots of different assessment tools and tests available if you would like to explore further. See Appendix B for more resources to get you started.

Chapter 7

Match Your Major to Your Personality

Nearly 2,500 years ago Aristotle recognized the inherent quality of human personality when he wrote, "All admit that, in a certain sense, the several kinds of character are bestowed by nature." Even then, in his Nicomachean Ethics, the Greek philosopher recognized that happiness is life's real goal and that neither wealth nor fame can ensure a happy life. Once you assess your personality type in this chapter, you will be able to match it to potential college majors and improve your chances of finding happiness in your chosen field.

Test Your Personality Traits

Are you spontaneous, cheerful, outgoing, and dependable? Perhaps you tend to be serious, modest, rigid, and orderly. Whether you're happy, anxious, solitary, conscientious, easy-going, determined, antagonistic, or flexible, you are composed of personality traits that make you one of a kind. Your personality traits influence how you live your life, from the way you interact with and perceive the world, to how you direct your energy, to how you make decisions.

While some educators think personality traits grow and change throughout one's life, others believe personality traits are consistent patterns that remain stable throughout one's life. Assessing your personality traits now will give you a snapshot in this moment in time, not a fixed profile. As with the other assessment tools in this book, it might be helpful to revisit this test periodically to see how you are changing and adapting to your personal, academic, and work environments.

Those who succeed within specific academic areas and within related careers may have certain personality characteristics in common. Personality traits can be thought of in many ways. Often people are described as extroverted or introverted, as structured or free, as qualitative or quantitative. Many labels are used to identify personalities. The adjectives you use to describe others, or that others use to describe you, reveal personal qualities, or personality traits. Are you outspoken or reserved, active or passive, expressive or stoic, athletic or intellectual? Some behaviors that come naturally for some are unnatural to others; these have an impact upon academic and career success and, therefore, should influence related choices.

An artistic person may find that majoring in mathematics doesn't add up. A numbers-cruncher can successfully complete art history and studio art classes, but majoring in drama may prove tragic. Who are you, and where will you thrive academically and vocationally? Will your personality influence your major choice, your academic performance, and your potential to excel within a career?

As you review the subsequent listings of careers and jobs, think about how people in these fields manifest their personalities on the job. Contemplate whether you judge yourself to be like these people and whether your personality is similar to theirs. Identifying criteria—including values, interests, and personality traits—will help you focus on major and career connections and allow you to declare a major and take academic and other steps toward career goals. As with all the assessments in this book, initial and honest impressions are all that is required to enhance self-knowledge and facilitate major decisions.

True-False Test of Personality

When I think of it in terms of my choice of college majors . . .

My personality is like an accountant's.

True					*False*
Always True	Often True	I Wish True	No Opinion	Often False	Always False

My personality is like an actor's.

True					*False*
Always True	Often True	I Wish True	No Opinion	Often False	Always False

My personality is like an actuary's.

True					*False*
Always True	Often True	I Wish True	No Opinion	Often False	Always False

My personality is like an administrative assistant's.

True					*False*
Always True	Often True	I Wish True	No Opinion	Often False	Always False

My personality is like an advertising account executive's.

True					*False*
Always True	Often True	I Wish True	No Opinion	Often False	Always False

My personality is like an advertising media planner's.

True					*False*
Always True	Often True	I Wish True	No Opinion	Often False	Always False

My personality is like an advertising sales executive's.

True					*False*
Always True	Often True	I Wish True	No Opinion	Often False	Always False

My personality is like an architect's.

True   *False*

| Always True | Often True | I Wish True | No Opinion | Often False | Always False |

My personality is like an art teacher's.

True   *False*

| Always True | Often True | I Wish True | No Opinion | Often False | Always False |

My personality is like an artist's.

True   *False*

| Always True | Often True | I Wish True | No Opinion | Often False | Always False |

My personality is like an athletic trainer's.

True   *False*

| Always True | Often True | I Wish True | No Opinion | Often False | Always False |

My personality is like an audiologist's.

True   *False*

| Always True | Often True | I Wish True | No Opinion | Often False | Always False |

My personality is like an automotive mechanic's.

True   *False*

| Always True | Often True | I Wish True | No Opinion | Often False | Always False |

My personality is like a biologist's.

True   *False*

| Always True | Often True | I Wish True | No Opinion | Often False | Always False |

My personality is like a broadcast journalist's.

True   *False*

| Always True | Often True | I Wish True | No Opinion | Often False | Always False |

My personality is like a carpenter's or a woodworker's.

True   *False*

| Always True | Often True | I Wish True | No Opinion | Often False | Always False |

My personality is like a chemist's.

True   *False*

Always True	Often True	I Wish True	No Opinion	Often False	Always False

My personality is like a child-care professional's.

True   *False*

Always True	Often True	I Wish True	No Opinion	Often False	Always False

My personality is like a coach's.

True   *False*

Always True	Often True	I Wish True	No Opinion	Often False	Always False

My personality is like a commercial banker's.

True   *False*

Always True	Often True	I Wish True	No Opinion	Often False	Always False

My personality is like a community service administrator's.

True   *False*

Always True	Often True	I Wish True	No Opinion	Often False	Always False

My personality is like a community service fundraiser's.

True   *False*

Always True	Often True	I Wish True	No Opinion	Often False	Always False

My personality is like a chef's.

True   *False*

Always True	Often True	I Wish True	No Opinion	Often False	Always False

My personality is like a chiropractor's.

True   *False*

Always True	Often True	I Wish True	No Opinion	Often False	Always False

My personality is like a college administrator's.

True   *False*

Always True	Often True	I Wish True	No Opinion	Often False	Always False

My personality is like a college faculty member's.

True   *False*

Always True   Often True   I Wish True   No Opinion   Often False   Always False

My personality is like a commercial or graphic artist's.

True   *False*

Always True   Often True   I Wish True   No Opinion   Often False   Always False

My personality is like a computer programmer's.

True   *False*

Always True   Often True   I Wish True   No Opinion   Often False   Always False

My personality is like a construction worker's.

True   *False*

Always True   Often True   I Wish True   No Opinion   Often False   Always False

My personality is like a dental assistant's.

True   *False*

Always True   Often True   I Wish True   No Opinion   Often False   Always False

My personality is like a dental hygienist's.

True   *False*

Always True   Often True   I Wish True   No Opinion   Often False   Always False

My personality is like a dentist's.

True   *False*

Always True   Often True   I Wish True   No Opinion   Often False   Always False

My personality is like a dietitian's.

True   *False*

Always True   Often True   I Wish True   No Opinion   Often False   Always False

My personality is like an elected office-holder's.

True   *False*

Always True   Often True   I Wish True   No Opinion   Often False   Always False

My personality is like an electrician's.

True   *False*

| Always True | Often True | I Wish True | No Opinion | Often False | Always False |

My personality is like an elementary education teacher's.

True   *False*

| Always True | Often True | I Wish True | No Opinion | Often False | Always False |

My personality is like an emergency medical technician's.

True   *False*

| Always True | Often True | I Wish True | No Opinion | Often False | Always False |

My personality is like an English teacher's.

True   *False*

| Always True | Often True | I Wish True | No Opinion | Often False | Always False |

My personality is like an engineer's.

True   *False*

| Always True | Often True | I Wish True | No Opinion | Often False | Always False |

My personality is like a flight attendant's.

True   *False*

| Always True | Often True | I Wish True | No Opinion | Often False | Always False |

My personality is like a florist's.

True   *False*

| Always True | Often True | I Wish True | No Opinion | Often False | Always False |

My personality is like a foreign language teacher's.

True   *False*

| Always True | Often True | I Wish True | No Opinion | Often False | Always False |

My personality is like a farmer's.

True   *False*

| Always True | Often True | I Wish True | No Opinion | Often False | Always False |

My personality is like a forester's.

True   *False*

| Always True | Often True | I Wish True | No Opinion | Often False | Always False |

My personality is like a gardener's.

True   *False*

| Always True | Often True | I Wish True | No Opinion | Often False | Always False |

My personality is like a geologist's.

True   *False*

| Always True | Often True | I Wish True | No Opinion | Often False | Always False |

My personality is like a guidance counselor's.

True   *False*

| Always True | Often True | I Wish True | No Opinion | Often False | Always False |

My personality is like a horticulturist's.

True   *False*

| Always True | Often True | I Wish True | No Opinion | Often False | Always False |

My personality is like a human resource professional's.

True   *False*

| Always True | Often True | I Wish True | No Opinion | Often False | Always False |

My personality is like an interior decorator's.

True   *False*

| Always True | Often True | I Wish True | No Opinion | Often False | Always False |

My personality is like an interior designer's.

True   *False*

| Always True | Often True | I Wish True | No Opinion | Often False | Always False |

My personality is like a investment banker's.

True   *False*

| Always True | Often True | I Wish True | No Opinion | Often False | Always False |

My personality is like an investment manager's.

True   *False*

| Always True | Often True | I Wish True | No Opinion | Often False | Always False |

My personality is like a lawyer's.

True   *False*

| Always True | Often True | I Wish True | No Opinion | Often False | Always False |

My personality is like a librarian's.

True   *False*

| Always True | Often True | I Wish True | No Opinion | Often False | Always False |

My personality is like a marketing professional's.

True   *False*

| Always True | Often True | I Wish True | No Opinion | Often False | Always False |

My personality is like a market researcher's.

True   *False*

| Always True | Often True | I Wish True | No Opinion | Often False | Always False |

My personality is like a mathematician's.

True   *False*

| Always True | Often True | I Wish True | No Opinion | Often False | Always False |

My personality is like a mathematics teacher's.

True   *False*

| Always True | Often True | I Wish True | No Opinion | Often False | Always False |

My personality is like a medical examiner's.

True   *False*

| Always True | Often True | I Wish True | No Opinion | Often False | Always False |

My personality is like a medical illustrator's.

True   *False*

| Always True | Often True | I Wish True | No Opinion | Often False | Always False |

My personality is like a medical technician's.

True   *False*

| Always True | Often True | I Wish True | No Opinion | Often False | Always False |

My personality is like a medical technologist's.

True   *False*

| Always True | Often True | I Wish True | No Opinion | Often False | Always False |

My personality is like a military officer's.

True   *False*

| Always True | Often True | I Wish True | No Opinion | Often False | Always False |

My personality is like that of military enlisted personnel.

True   *False*

| Always True | Often True | I Wish True | No Opinion | Often False | Always False |

My personality is like a minister's, a rabbi's, or a clergy member's.

True   *False*

| Always True | Often True | I Wish True | No Opinion | Often False | Always False |

My personality is like a mortgage banker's.

True   *False*

| Always True | Often True | I Wish True | No Opinion | Often False | Always False |

My personality is like a musician's.

True   *False*

| Always True | Often True | I Wish True | No Opinion | Often False | Always False |

My personality is like a music teacher's.

True   *False*

| Always True | Often True | I Wish True | No Opinion | Often False | Always False |

My personality is like a nurse's.

True   *False*

| Always True | Often True | I Wish True | No Opinion | Often False | Always False |

My personality is like a nursing-home professional's.

True   *False*

| Always True | Often True | I Wish True | No Opinion | Often False | Always False |

My personality is like an occupational therapist's.

True   *False*

| Always True | Often True | I Wish True | No Opinion | Often False | Always False |

My personality is like an optician's.

True   *False*

| Always True | Often True | I Wish True | No Opinion | Often False | Always False |

My personality is like an optometrist's.

True   *False*

| Always True | Often True | I Wish True | No Opinion | Often False | Always False |

My personality is like a paralegal's.

True   *False*

| Always True | Often True | I Wish True | No Opinion | Often False | Always False |

My personality is like a parks and recreation worker's.

True   *False*

| Always True | Often True | I Wish True | No Opinion | Often False | Always False |

My personality is like a physical education teacher's.

True   *False*

| Always True | Often True | I Wish True | No Opinion | Often False | Always False |

My personality is like a physical therapist's.

True   *False*

| Always True | Often True | I Wish True | No Opinion | Often False | Always False |

My personality is like a pharmacist's.

True   *False*

| Always True | Often True | I Wish True | No Opinion | Often False | Always False |

My personality is like a photographer's.

True   *False*

Always True	Often True	I Wish True	No Opinion	Often False	Always False

My personality is like a physician's.

True   *False*

Always True	Often True	I Wish True	No Opinion	Often False	Always False

My personality is like a plumber's or a plumbing contractor's.

True   *False*

Always True	Often True	I Wish True	No Opinion	Often False	Always False

My personality is like a police officer's or an investigator's.

True   *False*

Always True	Often True	I Wish True	No Opinion	Often False	Always False

My personality is like a psychologist's or a counselor's.

True   *False*

Always True	Often True	I Wish True	No Opinion	Often False	Always False

My personality is like a public relations professional's.

True   *False*

Always True	Often True	I Wish True	No Opinion	Often False	Always False

My personality is like a purchasing agent's.

True   *False*

Always True	Often True	I Wish True	No Opinion	Often False	Always False

My personality is like a radiology technician's.

True   *False*

Always True	Often True	I Wish True	No Opinion	Often False	Always False

My personality is like a real estate agent's.

True   *False*

Always True	Often True	I Wish True	No Opinion	Often False	Always False

My personality is like a real estate developer's.

True   *False*

| Always True | Often True | I Wish True | No Opinion | Often False | Always False |

My personality is like a reporter's or a journalist's.

True   *False*

| Always True | Often True | I Wish True | No Opinion | Often False | Always False |

My personality is like a research-and-development scientist's.

True   *False*

| Always True | Often True | I Wish True | No Opinion | Often False | Always False |

My personality is like a respiratory therapist's.

True   *False*

| Always True | Often True | I Wish True | No Opinion | Often False | Always False |

My personality is like a restaurant manager's.

True   *False*

| Always True | Often True | I Wish True | No Opinion | Often False | Always False |

My personality is like a retail manager's.

True   *False*

| Always True | Often True | I Wish True | No Opinion | Often False | Always False |

My personality is like a school administrator's.

True   *False*

| Always True | Often True | I Wish True | No Opinion | Often False | Always False |

My personality is like a science teacher's.

True   *False*

| Always True | Often True | I Wish True | No Opinion | Often False | Always False |

My personality is like a social studies teacher's.

True   *False*

| Always True | Often True | I Wish True | No Opinion | Often False | Always False |

My personality is like a sociologist's.

True   *False*

| Always True | Often True | I Wish True | No Opinion | Often False | Always False |

My personality is like a social worker's.

True   *False*

| Always True | Often True | I Wish True | No Opinion | Often False | Always False |

My personality is like a special education teacher's.

True   *False*

| Always True | Often True | I Wish True | No Opinion | Often False | Always False |

My personality is like a speech pathologist's and audiologist's.

True   *False*

| Always True | Often True | I Wish True | No Opinion | Often False | Always False |

My personality is like a systems analyst's.

True   *False*

| Always True | Often True | I Wish True | No Opinion | Often False | Always False |

My personality is like that of a teacher of English as a second language.

True   *False*

| Always True | Often True | I Wish True | No Opinion | Often False | Always False |

My personality is like a technical writer's.

True   *False*

| Always True | Often True | I Wish True | No Opinion | Often False | Always False |

My personality is like a translator's.

True   *False*

| Always True | Often True | I Wish True | No Opinion | Often False | Always False |

My personality is like a travel agent's.

True   *False*

| Always True | Often True | I Wish True | No Opinion | Often False | Always False |

My personality is like a veterinarian's.

True   *False*

| Always True | Often True | I Wish True | No Opinion | Often False | Always False |

This assessment gauges how you identify with the perceived personality traits of various fields of study and careers. After you've marked your responses on the test, look at your results. Highlight the answers you identified as "always true" and "often true." Take note of the ones you marked as "I wish true." Do you have any thoughts about why you wish you related to the personality traits related to these particular jobs?

The Myers-Briggs Type Indicator Chart

In the 1920s, psychoanalyst and Freudian disciple Carl Jung developed a theory of psychological types. Jung's work influenced the work of two American psychologists twenty years later. In 1947, Katherine Briggs and her daughter, Isabel Briggs-Myers, produced the Myers-Briggs Type Indicator (MBTI), documenting four personality preference scales and sixteen distinct personality types.

They used four basic aspects of personality to come up with their types, each rated on a continuum between opposites:

- Extraverted-Introverted: How we interact with the world and where we direct our energy
- Sensing-Intuitive: The kind of information we perceive naturally
- Thinking-Feeling: How we make decisions
- Judging-Perceiving: Whether we prefer to live in a structured way or spontaneously

Each combination of four letters in the following table represents one of the sixteen different personality types.

Myers-Briggs Codes, Careers, and Majors

ISTJ	ISFJ	INFJ	INTJ
Introverted Sensing Thinking Judging	Introverted Sensing Feeling Judging	Introverted Intuitive Feeling Judging	Introverted Intuitive Thinking Judging
Auditor, office manager, accountant, efficiency expert, insurance underwriter, insurance claims examiner, statistician, technical writer, real estate appraiser, police officer, detective, IRS agent, government worker, military officer, real estate agent, corrections officer, probation officer, architectural drafter, flight navigator, bank examiner, tax preparer, stock broker, estate planner, credit analyst, budget analyst, principal, teacher, librarian, legal researcher, engineer, mechanic, computer programmer, technical writer, paralegal, pharmaceutical sales rep, pharmaceutical researcher, EEG technologist, Web designer, systems engineer, veterinarian, surgeon, dentist, nurse, pharmacist, lab technician, medical researcher, physician, coroner, optometrist	Dental hygienist, family physician, nurse, physical therapist, health-care administrator, dietitian, optician, nutritionist, pharmacist, pharmacy technician, radiological technician respirator therapist, veterinarian, home health aide, medical and dental assistant, pharmaceutical sales rep, hospice worker, medical researcher, biologist, dentist, orthodontist, occupational therapist, biochemist, massage therapist, dental laboratory technician, dialysis technician, preschool teacher, librarian, social worker, counselor, speech pathologist, probation officer, elementary school teacher, special ed teacher, curator, guidance counselor, athletic trainer, game warden, residence counselor, farmer, customer service, personnel administrator, bookkeeper, paralegal, computer support, museum researcher, funeral director, interior decorator, electrician, retail entrepreneur, merchandiser, real estate agent	Career counselor, clinical psychologist, high school or college teacher, librarian, special ed teacher, bilingual teacher, substance abuse counselor, social worker, sociologist, museum researcher, occupational therapist, priest/clergy, artist, playwright, novelist, interior designer, media planner, editor, magazine art director, film editor, filmmaker, set designer, health-care administrator, social service director, mental health counselor, mediator, massage therapist, chiropractor, fundraising director, legislative aide, human resource manager, marketer, environmental lawyer, curator, and literary agent.	Management consultant, economist, pharmaceutical researcher, financial planner, investment banker, credit analyst, financial analyst, strategic planner, budget analyst, real estate appraiser, scientist, systems analyst, electrical technician, design engineer, astronomer, computer programmer, environmental planner, biomedical engineer, network and systems administrator, systems analyst, computer animator, LAN administrator, Web designer, business analyst, software developer, mathematics teacher, computer science teacher, anthropologist, curator, archivist, psychiatrist, psychologist, neurologist, cardiologist, pharmacologist, coroner, pathologist, geneticist, surgeon, attorney, investment analyst, judge, news writer, engineer, architect, environmental scientist, pilot, writer, editor, artist, inventor, graphic designer, art director
Architecture, business, biological sciences, computer programming, criminal justice, education, engineering, health sciences and allied health care, and library science.	Business, biological sciences, chemistry, computer programming, education, engineering, health sciences and allied health care, history, law and legal studies, library science, mental, social, and public health, nutrition science, and psychology	Art, biological sciences, chemistry education, engineering, English language and literature, health sciences and allied health care, history, library science, mental, social and, public health, nutrition science, and psychology	Art, business, biological sciences, chemistry, computer, science/information technology, computer programming, criminal justice, economics, education, engineering, health sciences and allied health care, history, law and legal studies, library science, mental health, social and public health, nutrition science, and psychology

ISTP	ISFP	INFP	INTP
Introverted Sensing Thinking Perceiving	Introverted Sensing Feeling Perceiving	Introverted Intuitive Feeling Perceiving	Introverted Intuitive Thinking Perceiving
Police and corrections officer, pilot, intelligence agent, firefighter, pharmaceutical sales, private investigator, coach, photographer, electrical, mechanical, and civil engineer, software developer, network specialist, computer programmer, marine biologist, systems analyst, geologist, EEG technician, emergency medical technician, dental assistant, surgical technician, emergency physician, securities analyst, purchasing agent, buyer, banker, economist, paralegal, management consultant, insurance adjuster, computer repair, airline mechanic, carpenter, commercial artist, landscape architect, forester, naturalist, television camera operator, military officer, air traffic controller	Fashion designer, carpenter, jeweler, gardener, painter, dancer, designer, chef, artist, tailor, nurse, physical therapist, massage therapist, radiology technician, medical assistant, dental hygienist and assistant, veterinary assistant, home health aide, primary care physician, nutritionist, optician, optometrist, physiologist, occupational therapist, art therapist, respiratory therapist, surgeon, personal trainer, veterinarian, speech pathologist, pharmacist, hospice worker, substance abuse counselor, surveyor, forester, botanist, geologist, mechanic, marine biologist, zoologist, archeologist, systems analyst, elementary science or art teacher, police and corrections officer, child welfare counselor, social worker, preschool teacher, special ed teacher, pilot, coach, firefighter, paralegal, insurance appraiser	Artist, writer, journalist, entertainer, architect, actor, editor, musician, film producer and/ or editor, interior designer, college humanities professor, researcher, clinical psychologist, counselor, social worker, librarian, special ed teacher, bilingual teacher, social worker, substance abuse counselor, translator and interpreter, career counselor, curator, minister/clergy, dietitian, physical therapist, occupational therapist, speech pathologist, holistic health practitioner, geneticist, ethicist, human resource specialist, conflict resolution consultant, organizational psychologist, labor relations specialist, corporate trainer, recruiter and educational software developer	Computer programmer, research and development, strategic planner, financial planner, investment banker, management information consultant, programmer, network administrator, analyst, Web developer, computer engineer, business analyst, software developer, neurologist, physicist, plastic surgeon, pharmacist, scientist, researcher, biomedical engineer, veterinarian, microbiologist, geneticist, lawyer, economist, psychologist, financial analyst, architect, intellectual property attorney, mediator, entrepreneur, venture capitalist, business analyst, agent, physicist, mathematician, archeologist, historian, philosopher, college professor, economist, photographer, creative writer, artist, entertainer, producer, editor
Business, biological sciences, chemistry, computer programming, criminal justice, education, engineering, health sciences and allied health care, history, law and legal studies, library science, mental health, social and public health, natural resources and conservation, nutrition science, and psychology	Art, biological sciences, communication and journalism, computer science, criminal justice, education, English language and literature, health sciences and allied health care, mental health, social and public health, psychology, therapy and rehabilitation	Art, business, biological sciences, chemistry, computer programming, criminal justice, education, engineering, English language and literature, health sciences and allied health care, history, law and legal studies, library science, mental health, social and public health, music, natural resources and conservation, nutrition science, psychology, therapy and rehabilitation	Archeology, business, biological, sciences, chemistry, computer programming, economics, engineering, health sciences and allied health care, history, law and legal studies, library science, mental health, social and public health, natural resources and conservation, nutrition science, psychology, therapy and rehabilitation

ESTP	ESFP	ENFP	ENTP
Extroverted Sensing Thinking Perceiving	Introverted Sensing Feeling Perceiving	Extroverted Intuitive Feeling Perceiving	Extroverted Intuitive Thinking Perceiving
Police officer, firefighter, paramedic, corrections officer, real estate agent, emergency medical technician, respiratory therapist, flight attendant, military officer, probation officer, insurance adjuster and examiner, personal financial planner, auditor, stockbroker, banker, insurance sales, budget analyst, sportscaster, reporter, radio/television personality, musician, actor, carpenter, farmer, chef, electrical engineer, civil engineer, industrial and mechanical engineer, EEG technician, radiological technician, marine biologist, loan manager, landscape architect, chiropractor, flight attendant, travel agent, real estate broker, entrepreneur, developer, retail salesperson, management consultant, claims adjuster	Early childhood educator, child-care provider, art, drama and music teacher, coach, substance abuse counselor, child welfare counselor, marine biologist, special education teacher, emergency room nurse, social worker, medical and dental assistant, nurse, physical therapist, nutritionist, optician and optometrist, pharmacy technician, veterinarian technician, occupational therapist, fitness trainer, hospice worker, podiatrist, speech pathologist, pediatrician, art therapist, chiropractor, photographer, film producer, special events coordinator, painter/artist, news reporter and anchor, actor, police officer, retail merchandiser, public relations specialist, fundraiser, insurance agent, real estate agent, landscape architect, chef, interior deliverer, recreational therapist, ecotourism specialist, environmental scientist, zoologist, marine biologist, geologist	Journalist, screenwriter, actor, musician, newscaster, interior decorator, artist, editor, creative director, filmmaker, public relations specialist, marketing consultant, advertising account executive, copywriter, strategic planner, publicist, research assistant, special education teacher, bilingual teacher, early childhood educator, substance abuse counselor, social worker, development director, career counselor, pastoral counselor, rehabilitation worker, social scientist, social psychologist, counseling psychologist, anthropologist, guidance counselor, dietician, speech pathologist, holistic health practitioner, massage therapist, physical therapist, legal mediator, chiropractor, urban and regional planner, occupational therapist, consultant, inventor, salesperson, restaurateur, public relations specialist, marketing, and recruiter	Entrepreneur, inventor, management consultant, venture capitalist, literary agent, journalist, actor, outplacement consultant, university president, attorney, securities and commodities sales, business manager, human resources recruiter, advertising creative director, public relations specialist, marketing, producer, Internet architect, creative writer, copy writer, reporter, news analyst, strategic planner, real estate agent, investment broker, computer analyst, financial planner, investment banker, urban planner, politician, political analyst, chiropractor, environmental scientist, and educational psychologist
Agriculture, business, biological sciences, communication and journalism, criminal justice, education, engineering, health sciences and allied health care, history, law and legal studies, library science, mental health, music, social and public health, theatre, natural resources and conservation, nutrition science, psychology	Art, business, biological sciences, communications and journalism, design, education, engineering, food and nutrition science, geology, health sciences and allied health care, health and fitness, mental health, social and public health, theatre, natural resources and conservation, nutrition science, psychology	Art, business, biological sciences, communications and journalism, design, education, geology, health sciences and allied health care, health and fitness, mental, social and public health, theatre, natural resources and conservation, nutrition science, psychology, therapy and rehabilitation	Business, biological sciences, communications and journalism, design, English language and literature, environmental studies, geology, health sciences and allied health care, law and legal studies and public health, theatre, natural resources and conservation, psychology, theatre, therapy and rehabilitation, urban and regional planning

ESTJ	ESFJ	ENFJ	ENTJ
Extroverted Sensing Thinking Judging	Extroverted Sensing Feeling Judging	Extroverted Intuitive Feeling Judging	Extroverted Intuitive Thinking Judging
Insurance agent, sales, military officer, pharmaceutical sales, police, probation and corrections officer, athletic coach and trainer, underwriter, budget analyst, airline pilot, paralegal, real estate appraiser, insurance adjuster, legislative assistant, recreational therapist, mechanical engineer, computer analyst, auditor, farmer, pharmacist, auditor, EEG technologist, paralegal, network administrator, purchasing agent, management consultant, bank manager, credit analyst, property manager, dentist, physician, stockbroker, judge, executive, electrical engineer, pharmacist, lawyer, principal, chief information officer	Medical and dental assistant, speech pathologist, family physician, nurse, dentist, nutritionist, massage therapist, optometrist and optician, pharmacist, veterinarian, respiratory therapist, physical therapist, primary care physician, personal trainer, chiropractor, dialysis technician, aerobics instructor, elementary school teacher, special ed teacher, child-care provider, coach, bilingual educator, principal, social worker, counselor, minister/clergy, legislative assistant, paralegal, public relations account executive, loan officer, sales rep, retail owner, insurance agent, credit counselor, property manager, real estate appraiser, flight attendant, customer service rep, fundraiser, travel agent, real estate agent, and caterer	Advertising account executive, public relations specialist, writer and/or journalist, entertainer, artist, fundraiser, recruiter, newscaster, politician, editor, graphic artist, reporter, psychologist, career counselor, clergy/ministry, interpreter and translator, guidance counselor, teacher, college professor, dean of students, librarian, social worker, nonprofit director, special ed teacher, bilingual educator, social worker, planned giving officer, college administrator, urban and regional planner, sociologist, adult day-care professional, holistic health practitioner, dietitian, chiropractor, sales trainer, personnel recruiter, travel agent, sales manager, advertising account executive, special event planner	Business executive, personnel manager, sales manager, college administrator, managing editor, retail manager, real estate manager, personal financial planner, economic analyst, mortgage broker, investment banker, stockbroker, economist, treasurer, venture capitalist, business consultant, labor relations manager, legislative assistant, political consultant, attorney, judge, psychologist, science and social science teacher, chemical engineer, biomedical engineer, psychiatrist, pathologist, pilot, network administrator, systems administrator
Business, biological sciences, chemistry, computer programming, criminal justice, education, engineering, health sciences and allied health care, history, law and legal studies, library science, mental health, social and public health, natural resources and conservation, nutrition science, psychology	Business, biological sciences, chemistry, computer programming, criminal justice, education, health sciences and allied health care, history, law and legal studies, library science, mental health, social and public health, natural resources and conservation, nutrition science and psychology	Art, business, programming, criminal justice, education, English language and literature, health sciences and allied health, health and human services, history, law and legal studies, mental health, social and public health, natural resources and conservation, nutrition science, psychology, religious studies and theological studies, therapy and rehabilitation	Business, biological sciences, communications and journalism, computer science, economics, English language and literature, engineering, environmental studies, geology, health sciences and allied health care, law and legal studies and public health, theatre, natural resources and conservation, psychology, theatre, therapy and rehabilitation

You can find volumes detailing each of these personality types. Other resources index careers using the Myers-Briggs Type Indicator codes as well.

Personality and Majors

To analyze the results of your true-false personality test, complete the following Personality Grid. Refer to the table of Myers-Briggs codes (pages 144–47), the appendices, and other resources mentioned in this book for help.

College Major Personality Grid

Personality Matches Ranked in Order of Significance "Always true" and "often true" personality matches that must be incorporated into major and career decisions, listed in order of significance.	**Potential Courses, Majors, and Job Titles** Use Chapter 9 information, easily identifiable associations between true-false statements and majors, as well as a course catalog to identify courses, majors, and job titles you believe are associated with each field.
1.	
2.	
3.	
4.	
5.	
6.	
7.	
8.	
9	
10.	
Describe why you listed your top three personality matches above and identify majors associated with these options:	
Note the Myers-Briggs code that you think best describes you and identify majors associated with this code:	

"I Wish True" Personality Matches in Order of Significance	Potential Courses, Majors, and Careers Courses, majors, and careers you believe are associated with each matching field or job.
1.	
2.	
3.	
4.	
5.	

Describe why you wish your top two personality matches were true:

Myers-Briggs Codes, Majors, and Careers Grid

Using Web-based or other assessments, identify your Myers-Briggs code and
most significant options for major and career

ISTJ *Introverted Sensing Thinking Judging*	**ISFJ** *Introverted Sensing Feeling Judging*	**INFJ** *Introverted Intuitive Feeling Judging*	**INTJ** *Introverted Intuitive Thinking Judging*
Top Three Career Options	**Top Three Career Options**	**Top Three Career Options**	**Top Three Career Options**
1.	1.	1.	1.
2.	2.	2.	2.
3.	3.	3.	3.
Top Three Major Options	**Top Three Major Options**	**Top Three Major Options**	**Top Three Major Options**
1.	1.	1.	1.
2.	2.	2.	2.
3.	3.	3.	3.
ISTP *Introverted Sensing Thinking Perceiving*	**ISFP** *Introverted Sensing Feeling Perceiving*	**INFP** *Introverted Intuitive Feeling Perceiving*	**INTP** *Introverted Intuitive Thinking Perceiving*
Top Three Career Options	**Top Three Career Options**	**Top Three Career Options**	**Top Three Career Options**
1.	1.	1.	1.
2.	2.	2.	2.
3.	3.	3.	3.
Top Three Major Options	**Top Three Major Options**	**Top Three Major Options**	**Top Three Major Options**
1.	1.	1.	1.
2.	2.	2.	2.
3.	3.	3.	3.
ESTP *Extroverted Sensing Thinking Perceiving*	**ESFP** *Introverted Sensing Feeling Perceiving*	**ENFP** *Extroverted Intuitive Feeling Perceiving*	**ENTP** *Extroverted Intuitive Thinking Perceiving*
Top Three Career Options	**Top Three Career Options**	**Top Three Career Options**	**Top Three Career Options**
1.	1.	1.	1.
2.	2.	2.	2.
3.	3.	3.	3.
Top Three Major Options	**Top Three Major Options**	**Top Three Major Options**	**Top Three Major Options**
1.	1.	1.	1.
2.	2.	2.	2.
3.	3.	3.	3.

ESTJ *Extroverted Sensing Thinking Judging*	ESFJ *Extroverted Sensing Feeling Judging*	ENFJ *Extroverted Intuitive Feeling Judging*	ENTJ *Extroverted Intuitive Thinking Judging*
Top Three Career Options	**Top Three Career Options**	**Top Three Career Options**	**Top Three Career Options**
1.	1.	1.	1.
2.	2.	2.	2.
3.	3.	3.	3.
Top Three Major Options	**Top Three Major Options**	**Top Three Major Options**	**Top Three Major Options**
1.	1.	1.	1.
2.	2.	2.	2.
3.	3.	3.	3.

Compare with "always true" personality matches, then identify your top five career options:
1.
2.
3
4.
5.

Compare with "always true" personality matches, then identify your top five major options:
1.
2.
3
4.
5.

It's considered unethical to administer an MBTI assessment without a follow-up verification session with a qualified professional. Therefore, the self-administered personality inventories found in books and online are approximations of the real thing. If you would like to continue your research into personality assessment, Appendix B includes the resources to get you started.

Chapter 8

Match Your Major to Your Skills

The Roman poet Sextus Propertius (49–15 B.C.) wrote, "Let each man pass his days in that wherein his skill is greatest." You may choose a major that matches your interests, values, and personality, but in order to succeed in the course-work and related professions, it helps to have the right skills. The good news is that, unlike core personality traits, skills can be learned and improved. In this chapter you'll discover the skills you already possess, as well as those you'd like to develop.

Test Your Skills

Perhaps someone has complimented you on your writing or public speaking ability. Or maybe you excel at negotiating, researching, or making decisions. Are your powers of persuasion so great that people say you could sell refrigerators at the North Pole? Maybe you are a great coach, reporter, or listener. These are just a few of the skills that you might need, depending on which major you choose. You may have an innate ability for any of these skills, or you may have to work hard to do them well. This true-false test will provide you with a current picture of your aptitude for over 100 skills, from managing time to evaluating groups. If you decide on a major that requires skills that you don't have, your diligence and desire to succeed will help you acquire them. Work through the test now.

True-False Test of Skills
I would like to use the following skills in my chosen major or career.

Planning and Organizational Skills

I want to meet deadlines and manage time effectively.

True   *False*

| Always True | Often True | I Wish True | No Opinion | Often False | Always False |

I want to work under time and environmental pressures.

True   *False*

| Always True | Often True | I Wish True | No Opinion | Often False | Always False |

I want to successfully juggle multiple demands and competing projects.

True   *False*

| Always True | Often True | I Wish True | No Opinion | Often False | Always False |

I want to identify and prioritize things to be accomplished.

True   *False*

| Always True | Often True | I Wish True | No Opinion | Often False | Always False |

I want to assess, prioritize, and act upon the needs of myself and/or others.

True   *False*

| Always True | Often True | I Wish True | No Opinion | Often False | Always False |

I want to develop goals for myself and/or an organization.

True   *False*

| Always True | Often True | I Wish True | No Opinion | Often False | Always False |

I want to work effectively with organization members to plan and complete tasks or projects.

True   *False*

| Always True | Often True | I Wish True | No Opinion | Often False | Always False |

I want to follow up with others to evaluate the progress of tasks and present their status to others.

True   *False*

| Always True | Often True | I Wish True | No Opinion | Often False | Always False |

I want to persevere with a difficult endeavor and see it through to completion.

True   *False*

| Always True | Often True | I Wish True | No Opinion | Often False | Always False |

Performance and Presentation Skills

I want to sing, dance, act, or perform for an audience.

True   *False*

| Always True | Often True | I Wish True | No Opinion | Often False | Always False |

I want to regularly speak to large groups.

True   *False*

| Always True | Often True | I Wish True | No Opinion | Often False | Always False |

I want to regularly speak to small groups.

True   *False*

| Always True | Often True | I Wish True | No Opinion | Often False | Always False |

I want to conduct presentations that are required for others to complete specific tasks.

True   *False*

| Always True | Often True | I Wish True | No Opinion | Often False | Always False |

I want to conduct presentations used to motivate others.

True   *False*

| Always True | Often True | I Wish True | No Opinion | Often False | Always False |

I want to conduct presentations to educate others regarding
specific concepts, terms, or approaches.

True   *False*

| Always True | Often True | I Wish True | No Opinion | Often False | Always False |

Critical-Thinking Skills

I want to quickly and accurately identifying key issues when
making a decision or solving a problem.

True   *False*

| Always True | Often True | I Wish True | No Opinion | Often False | Always False |

I want to identify general principles that explain data or human behavior.

True   *False*

| Always True | Often True | I Wish True | No Opinion | Often False | Always False |

I want to examine the assumptions underlying analyses or conclusions.

True   *False*

| Always True | Often True | I Wish True | No Opinion | Often False | Always False |

I want to recognize the relationships among information obtained from diverse sources.

True   *False*

| Always True | Often True | I Wish True | No Opinion | Often False | Always False |

I want to use facts to judge the validity of theories.

True   *False*

| Always True | Often True | I Wish True | No Opinion | Often False | Always False |

I want to create innovative solutions to complex problems.

True   *False*

| Always True | Often True | I Wish True | No Opinion | Often False | Always False |

I want to critically evaluate theories and research, apply the results in
the solution of problems, and present my conclusions.

True   *False*

| Always True | Often True | I Wish True | No Opinion | Often False | Always False |

Leadership, Human Relations, and Interpersonal Skills

I want to maintain group cooperation and support in my role as a motivational leader.

True   *False*

| Always True | Often True | I Wish True | No Opinion | Often False | Always False |

I want to keep a group on track when working toward a goal in my role as a logistical leader.

True   *False*

| Always True | Often True | I Wish True | No Opinion | Often False | Always False |

I want to interact and work effectively with peers, superiors, and subordinates.

True   *False*

| Always True | Often True | I Wish True | No Opinion | Often False | Always False |

I want to interact with and appreciate people from diverse cultural, social, ethnic, and religious backgrounds.

True   *False*

| Always True | Often True | I Wish True | No Opinion | Often False | Always False |

I want to communicate effectively and sensitively to individuals and groups situations, orally and in writing.

True   *False*

| Always True | Often True | I Wish True | No Opinion | Often False | Always False |

I want to teach or train others in a skill, concept, or principle.

True   *False*

| Always True | Often True | I Wish True | No Opinion | Often False | Always False |

I want to demonstrate effective social behavior in a variety of settings and circumstances.

True   *False*

| Always True | Often True | I Wish True | No Opinion | Often False | Always False |

I want to effectively collaborate with others to complete projects or reach goals.

True   *False*

| Always True | Often True | I Wish True | No Opinion | Often False | Always False |

I want to delegate tasks and responsibilities to others.

True   *False*

| Always True | Often True | I Wish True | No Opinion | Often False | Always False |

I want to be part of a team that works on diverse assignments.

True   *False*

| Always True | Often True | I Wish True | No Opinion | Often False | Always False |

Oral and Written Communication Skills

I want to organize and present ideas effectively for
formal and spontaneous speeches, classes, or training.

True   *False*

| Always True | Often True | I Wish True | No Opinion | Often False | Always False |

I want to effectively facilitate and participate in group discussions and to brainstorm ideas.

True   *False*

| Always True | Often True | I Wish True | No Opinion | Often False | Always False |

I want to debate issues while respecting the opinions of others.

True   *False*

| Always True | Often True | I Wish True | No Opinion | Often False | Always False |

I want to read and condense large amounts of material.

True   *False*

| Always True | Often True | I Wish True | No Opinion | Often False | Always False |

I want to write clear, grammatical, concise, objective, and convincing reports in appropriate formats.

True   *False*

| Always True | Often True | I Wish True | No Opinion | Often False | Always False |

I want to write and speak effectively in a second language.

True   *False*

| Always True | Often True | I Wish True | No Opinion | Often False | Always False |

I want to deliver clear and persuasive verbal presentations .

True   *False*

| Always True | Often True | I Wish True | No Opinion | Often False | Always False |

I want to express and defend ideas in a clear, objective, nonjudgmental manner.

True   *False*

| Always True | Often True | I Wish True | No Opinion | Often False | Always False |

I want to use print, Web-based, and graphic resources for public relations, promotions, and event-planning efforts.

True   *False*

| Always True | Often True | I Wish True | No Opinion | Often False | Always False |

I want to use various media to present ideas effectively and/or imaginatively.

True   *False*

| Always True | Often True | I Wish True | No Opinion | Often False | Always False |

I want to use courteous telephone skills.

True   *False*

| Always True | Often True | I Wish True | No Opinion | Often False | Always False |

I want to use effective customer-service, mediation, and problem-solving skills.

True   *False*

| Always True | Often True | I Wish True | No Opinion | Often False | Always False |

I want to think, act, or make presentations effectively and with limited preparation.

True   *False*

| Always True | Often True | I Wish True | No Opinion | Often False | Always False |

Research, Investigation, and Presentation Skills

I want to use a variety of sources of information to research problems or answers to questions.

True   *False*

| Always True | Often True | I Wish True | No Opinion | Often False | Always False |

I want to conduct literature searches using Web-based resources.

True   *False*

| Always True | Often True | I Wish True | No Opinion | Often False | Always False |

I want to conduct literature searches using library-based printed resources.

True   *False*

| Always True | Often True | I Wish True | No Opinion | Often False | Always False |

I want to develop and test research questions and hypotheses.

True   *False*

| Always True | Often True | I Wish True | No Opinion | Often False | Always False |

I want to apply a variety of research methods to test the validity of data.

True   *False*

| Always True | Often True | I Wish True | No Opinion | Often False | Always False |

I want to design an experiment, theory, or model that effectively defines a problem.

True   *False*

| Always True | Often True | I Wish True | No Opinion | Often False | Always False |

I want to construct, administer, and interpret questionnaires or surveys.

True   *False*

| Always True | Often True | I Wish True | No Opinion | Often False | Always False |

I want to ethically recruit and treat research subjects.

True   *False*

| Always True | Often True | I Wish True | No Opinion | Often False | Always False |

I want to select appropriate statistical tests for the analysis of research.

True   *False*

| Always True | Often True | I Wish True | No Opinion | Often False | Always False |

I want to analyze and interpret statistical data.

True   *False*

| Always True | Often True | I Wish True | No Opinion | Often False | Always False |

I want to interpret qualitative and quantitative data.

True   *False*

| Always True | Often True | I Wish True | No Opinion | Often False | Always False |

I want to use computers or laboratory equipment to conduct and support research.

True   *False*

| Always True | Often True | I Wish True | No Opinion | Often False | Always False |

I want to select, administer, score, and interpret various psychological tests or assessments.

True   *False*

| Always True | Often True | I Wish True | No Opinion | Often False | Always False |

I want to deal effectively with financial, chronological, and logistical constraints on research.

True   *False*

| Always True | Often True | I Wish True | No Opinion | Often False | Always False |

I want to present findings of research efforts in graphic, text, and verbal formats.

True   *False*

| Always True | Often True | I Wish True | No Opinion | Often False | Always False |

Computer Skills

I want to use computer software to prepare reports, graphs, brochures, and Web pages and to conduct research.

True   *False*

| Always True | Often True | I Wish True | No Opinion | Often False | Always False |

I want to use software like Microsoft Word, Excel, and PowerPoint to complete tasks and projects.

True   *False*

| Always True | Often True | I Wish True | No Opinion | Often False | Always False |

I want to conduct Internet research and use e-mail skills.

True   *False*

| Always True | Often True | I Wish True | No Opinion | Often False | Always False |

I want to participate in computer programming and beta testing.

True   *False*

| Always True | Often True | I Wish True | No Opinion | Often False | Always False |

I want to use Web-page and Web-site design skills.

True   *False*

| Always True | Often True | I Wish True | No Opinion | Often False | Always False |

I want to repair or install computer hardware, software, or systems.

True   *False*

| Always True | Often True | I Wish True | No Opinion | Often False | Always False |

I want to serve as a technical liaison or in user-support capacities.

True   *False*

| Always True | Often True | I Wish True | No Opinion | Often False | Always False |

Personal Skills

I want to practice, define, and motivate ethical behavior.

True   *False*

| Always True | Often True | I Wish True | No Opinion | Often False | Always False |

I want to be able to tolerate stress and ambiguity.

True   *False*

Always True	Often True	I Wish True	No Opinion	Often False	Always False

I want to demonstrate flexibility and the ability to handle change.

True   *False*

Always True	Often True	I Wish True	No Opinion	Often False	Always False

I want to seek opportunities for professional development.

True   *False*

Always True	Often True	I Wish True	No Opinion	Often False	Always False

I want to identify personal values and apply them when making decisions.

True   *False*

Always True	Often True	I Wish True	No Opinion	Often False	Always False

I want to study or examine data, individuals, or objects using scientific, statistical, or theoretical models.

True   *False*

Always True	Often True	I Wish True	No Opinion	Often False	Always False

I want to examine, evaluate, and diagnose patients or clients.

True   *False*

Always True	Often True	I Wish True	No Opinion	Often False	Always False

I want to gain information via interviewing and questioning other people.

True   *False*

Always True	Often True	I Wish True	No Opinion	Often False	Always False

Quantitative, Financial, and Statistical Skills

I want to develop, monitor, and/or balance budgets.

True   *False*

Always True	Often True	I Wish True	No Opinion	Often False	Always False

I want to calculate, compute, analyze, and resolve numerical or quantitative audits or queries.

True   *False*

| Always True | Often True | I Wish True | No Opinion | Often False | Always False |

I want to review and analyze annual reports, financial statements, and other statistics.

True   *False*

| Always True | Often True | I Wish True | No Opinion | Often False | Always False |

I want to complete financial analyses, profit-and-loss projections, and other analyses.

True   *False*

| Always True | Often True | I Wish True | No Opinion | Often False | Always False |

I want to serve in an auditing and ledger-balancing role.

True   *False*

| Always True | Often True | I Wish True | No Opinion | Often False | Always False |

I want to develop and implement research studies.

True   *False*

| Always True | Often True | I Wish True | No Opinion | Often False | Always False |

I want to analyze data and present findings in graphic and text formats.

True   *False*

| Always True | Often True | I Wish True | No Opinion | Often False | Always False |

I want to analyze portfolios and make recommendations regarding investments.

True   *False*

| Always True | Often True | I Wish True | No Opinion | Often False | Always False |

I want to assess financial risk for clients or institutions.

True   *False*

| Always True | Often True | I Wish True | No Opinion | Often False | Always False |

I want to collect and analyze marketing research and/or sales data.

True   *False*

| Always True | Often True | I Wish True | No Opinion | Often False | Always False |

I want to collect and analyze opinion-survey data.

True   *False*

| Always True | Often True | I Wish True | No Opinion | Often False | Always False |

Sales, Marketing, Promotions, and Public Relations Skills

I want to plan and implement strategies or logistics for special events or campaigns.

True   *False*

| Always True | Often True | I Wish True | No Opinion | Often False | Always False |

I want to address customer inquiries and make presentations on the qualities of my product/service.

True   *False*

| Always True | Often True | I Wish True | No Opinion | Often False | Always False |

I want to address customer inquiries and present product/service qualities over the phone

True   *False*

| Always True | Often True | I Wish True | No Opinion | Often False | Always False |

I want to promote a person, organization, product, or service.

True   *False*

| Always True | Often True | I Wish True | No Opinion | Often False | Always False |

I want to raise money for an individual or institution.

True   *False*

| Always True | Often True | I Wish True | No Opinion | Often False | Always False |

I want to solicit and/or motivate volunteers.

True   *False*

| Always True | Often True | I Wish True | No Opinion | Often False | Always False |

I want to develop promotional or sales materials, correspondence, brochures, or Web presentations.

True   *False*

| Always True | Often True | I Wish True | No Opinion | Often False | Always False |

I want to address crises.

True   *False*

| Always True | Often True | I Wish True | No Opinion | Often False | Always False |

I want to interact with the press and/or seek press coverage for an individual or institution.

True   *False*

| Always True | Often True | I Wish True | No Opinion | Often False | Always False |

I want to evaluate the effectiveness of a campaign, advertisement, or event.

True   *False*

| Always True | Often True | I Wish True | No Opinion | Often False | Always False |

I want to make persuasive presentations or pitches.

True   *False*

| Always True | Often True | I Wish True | No Opinion | Often False | Always False |

I want to do cold calling on prospective buyers or clients.

True   *False*

| Always True | Often True | I Wish True | No Opinion | Often False | Always False |

Teaching, Counseling, and Therapy Skills

I want to solicit and listen to other people's expressions of feelings and/or frustrations.

True   *False*

| Always True | Often True | I Wish True | No Opinion | Often False | Always False |

I want to empathize and provide feedback regarding feelings, problems, or developmental issues.

True   *False*

| Always True | Often True | I Wish True | No Opinion | Often False | Always False |

I want to facilitate my own and other people's personal growth, insight, or developmental progress.

True   *False*

| Always True | Often True | I Wish True | No Opinion | Often False | Always False |

I want to advise or coach students, employees, or clients.

True   *False*

| Always True | Often True | I Wish True | No Opinion | Often False | Always False |

I want to defuse anger and mediate conflicts.

True   *False*

| Always True | Often True | I Wish True | No Opinion | Often False | Always False |

I want to measure other people's proficiency, status, or knowledge in a particular subject or skill set.

True   *False*

| Always True | Often True | I Wish True | No Opinion | Often False | Always False |

I want to mentor peers or subordinates.

True   *False*

| Always True | Often True | I Wish True | No Opinion | Often False | Always False |

I want to evaluate individuals or groups

True   *False*

| Always True | Often True | I Wish True | No Opinion | Often False | Always False |

Review your test. Highlight your "always true" and "often true" responses. These represent the skills you feel you have now. Note the statements you marked as "I wish true." These are the skills you would like to enhance. Think about why you wish you had these skills. Is it because they're used in a career you're contemplating? You can approach your results in two ways.

- You can identify majors that make use of the skills you already have, and narrow down your choices to ones that match your interests, personality, and values.
- You can identify majors that appeal to your personality, interests, and values, and decide to acquire or improve the skills you need to succeed at one of them.

Either way, once you've made a decision, you can immediately begin to set and implement the strategies to get you there. Don't forget that internships, externships, minors, and course clusters can be used to develop skills that aren't necessarily part of your major.

Skills and Majors

Of the four factors that come into play in choosing a major—interests, values, personality traits, and skills—skills will probably have the most impact on your future academic success. Highlight your top ten skills from the test and write them in the Skills Grid. Be sure to list your top five "I wish true" skills. Even though you may not possess these skills now, they could represent subject areas you feel passionate about or that closely match your values or personality.

College Major Skills Grid

Skills Statements Ranked in Order of Significance	How Skills Could Be Incorporated	Potential Courses, Majors, and Careers
"Always true" and "often true" skills that must be incorporated into decisions, listed in order of significance.	Ways each statement can be applied to academic or career contexts.	Courses, majors, and careers you believe are associated with each skills statement.
1.		
2.		
3.		
4.		
5.		
6.		
7.		
8.		
9.		
10.		

The five most significant skills that motivate my exploration of majors and careers:

1.

2.

3.

4.

5.

"I Wish True" Skills Statements in Order of Significance	How Skills Could Be Enhanced	Potential Courses, Majors, and Careers
Ways you can nurture each skill, including courses, seminars, and internships.	Courses, majors, and careers you believe associated with each skills statement.	
1.		
2.		
3.		
4.		
5.		
The three most significant skills that I wish to enhance:		
1.		
2.		
3.		
Describe why you wish to enhance those skills:		

Career Interests	Skills Connected to Interests
List five career fields you are curious about or are actively exploring.	Review the Chapter 4 true-false test and identify three skills statements you most associate with these careers.
1.	1. 2. 3.
2.	1. 2. 3.
3.	1. 2. 3.
4.	1. 2. 3.
5.	1. 2. 3.

Now, having completed the four true-false tests and grids that identify values, interests, personality traits, and skills, you should have a strong sense of self and more than simple impressions regarding potential majors. Before you tackle the majors and careers summary worksheets, checklists, and matrix presented in Chapter 10, take another look at what you've done so far:

- What do these documents reveal?
- Particularly, what do the three skills-focused grids identify?
- Can you identify and prioritize "top major option?" and "top potential careers?"

The Campbell Interest and Skill Survey

You're now familiar with the Holland vocational types, the Myers-Briggs personality types, and the Strong Inventory of Interests. One more test could be helpful to you as you make your decision about a major: the Campbell Interest and Skill Survey (CISS). While similar to other self-reported interest and skill inventories, the CISS also measures your confidence in your ability to perform activities related to various jobs. This instrument is most appropriate for students in or planning to attend college, for it focuses on careers that require some post-secondary education. The test's seven orientation scales and twenty-five basic scales correspond generally to the RIASEC themes associated with the Holland codes. The CISS basic scales are the following:

- **Influencing:** Leadership, law/politics, public speaking, sales, advertising/marketing
- **Organizing:** Supervision, financial services, office practices
- **Helping:** Adult development, counseling, child development, religious activities, medical practice
- **Creating:** Art/design, performing arts, writing, international activities, fashion, culinary arts
- **Analyzing:** Mathematics, science

- **Producing:** Mechanical crafts, woodworking, farming/forestry, plants/gardens, animal care
- **Adventuring:** Athletics/physical fitness, military/law enforcement, risks/adventure

Careers have long been indexed using the CISS, Myers-Briggs, and Holland codes. All of that information, plus your top ten skills as discovered through the true-false skills test, will help you focus your research on majors and careers and eventually make a decision with confidence. The seventeenth-century English poet George Herbert once wrote, "Skill and confidence are an unconquered army." Use all of the ordnance at your disposal, and set your sights on achievable goals.

Be sure to take the time to complete the Skills Grid on page 168. It will help you summarize and clarify your thoughts. Refer to the resources in the appendices to match majors and courses with particular skills.

Chapter 9

IQ: Intelligent Questions to Ask about Your Major

Eighteenth-century scientist Georg Christoph Lichtenberg once wrote, "One's first step in wisdom is to question everything." As you take the self-assessment tests and start to research the majors that interest you the most, compile a list of the questions. Every answer you find will lead to more questions—and that's a good thing. No less a luminary than Albert Einstein once said, "The important thing is not to stop questioning." If asking questions was good enough for him, it won't do you any harm to follow suit.

A Different Kind of IQ Test

No single publication comprehensively lists all possible majors or careers. The U.S. Department of Labor's Dictionary of Occupational Titles tries, but it's a laborious tome to use, and many of its entries aren't realistic or appropriate for college graduates. But there are plenty of other abbreviated and easy-to-use resources, such as those listed in Appendix B. They, and the exercises in this chapter, will help you further prioritize your options and zero in on a major.

On this test, the "Fields" and "Functions" columns contain entry-level options for pending and recent graduates. The column labeled "Majors and Academic Strategies" identifies those majors, minors, clusters, and postbaccalaureate course recommendations that relate to particular fields or job functions.

As you read through this College Major IQ Test, use a highlighter to mark entries and academic strategies that interest you. You'll link potential majors to careers by identifying fields, functions, and firms that appeal to you. As before, don't try to overanalyze each subject; just note your first impressions. You aren't committing to anything—yet.

College Major IQ Test

Review all columns from left to right and highlight the fields, functions, firms, majors, and academic strategies that are most appealing to you. Take into account all the insight you've gained from the earlier true-false tests of values, interests, personality traits, and skills.

Fields	Functions *Typical Entry-Level Jobs*	Firms *Where to Apply for Internships and After-Graduation Jobs*	Majors, and Academic Strategies *Potential Majors and More*
Accounting	Public accounting, private accounting, governmental accounting, internal auditing, bookkeeping, tax advisor	Public accounting firms; corporations; federal, state and local governments; nonprofit agencies; educational institutions	Accounting (major or minor); three-course accounting cluster consisting of two accounting courses (financial and managerial) plus economics, mathematics, or computer science; business major or minor; any major plus a masters in accounting; any major plus three to six post-baccalaureate courses
Advertising	Account management, media planning, creative market research, traffic production, media sales	National, regional, or local agencies; market research firms, print and broadcast media	Major or minor in advertising, marketing, business, economics, or communications; three-course marketing cluster; three-course advertising cluster for majors in psychology, sociology, anthropology, or English with an advertising and a marketing course; any major plus two to four post-baccalaureate courses
Aerospace and defense	Engineering, project management, sales, technical writing, contract development and pricing, auditing and budget analysis, quality assurance	Manufacturers, government agencies, consulting firms, educational institutions, think tanks	Majors in engineering or computer science; three-course engineering cluster consisting of business, management, or economics; any major plus three to six post-baccalaureate courses

Banking	Investment banking, commercial banking, corporate finance, sales and trading, merger and acquisitions, research, loan officer, branch management, internal audit, regulatory affairs, trust, mortgage banking, institutional sales	Commercial banks, investment banks, mortgage banks, savings and loans, home lenders	Major or minor in business, economics, mathematics, computer science, or finance; three-course cluster of accounting, finance, and management courses; any major plus two accounting and two finance or economics courses; master's in accounting; master's in management; master's in business administration; any major plus three to four post-baccalaureate courses
Biotech and pharmaceutical	Laboratory scientist, laboratory technician, quality assurance, sales and marketing, regulatory affairs, research and development, project management, statistician, operations, finance and management	Pharmaceutical firms, biotech companies, educational institutions, government agencies	Major or minor in biomedicine, biology, biochemistry, chemistry, or science; three-course biology cluster; three-course biochemistry or chemistry cluster; any major plus three to six post-baccalaureate courses in business, economics, or mathematics and two chemistry or biology courses
Consumer brand management and marketing	Brand manager, marketing assistant, marketing research, promotions and public relations, merchandising, advertising, sales analysis and forecasting	Manufacturers, advertising agencies, marketing consulting firms, public relations firms, retailers	Major or minor in advertising, marketing, business, economics, or communications; three-course marketing cluster; three-course advertising cluster; major in psychology, sociology, anthropology or English plus two courses in accounting marketing and management; any major plus two to four post-baccalaureate courses
Education	Teacher, librarian, coach, counselor, child-care and early childhood education, admissions, academic advising, researcher	Private and public preschools, private and public K–12 schools, private and public colleges, private and public universities, educational consulting firms, government agencies, human and social service agencies, rehabilitation agencies and homes	Major or minor in education, library sciences, counseling, or psychology; three-course counseling and psychology clusters; master's in teaching; certification programs

Energy	Oil and gas exploration, commodity trading, research and development, alternative energy, lobbying, regulatory and policy, retail provider	Oil and gas manufacturers, oil and gas distributors, equipment suppliers, government agencies, consulting firms, retailers	Major or minor in biomedicine, biology, biochemistry, chemistry or science; three-course biology cluster; three-course biochemistry or chemistry cluster; any major plus three to six post-baccalaureate courses; major in business, economics, or mathematics plus two chemistry or biology courses
Fashion and merchandising	Design, promotions and publicity, sales and buying, photography, event planning, manufacturing and distribution	Designers and manufacturers, retailers, publications, public relations firms, advertising agencies	Major or minor in fashion design or fashion merchandising; major in communications or marketing and two design or merchandising courses; design, studio arts, or related major; three-course merchandising or design cluster; any major plus two to six post-baccalaureate courses
Financial services	Broker/salesperson, private client/private banker, investment/equities analyst, bond analyst/rater, credit card services, institutional sales, investment/retirement planner/advisor, operations, information technology, mutual fund manager, hedge fund manager	Financial services firms, insurance companies, online brokerage firms, commercial banks, private banks, investment banks, savings and loans	Major or minor in business, economics, mathematics, computer science, or finance; three-course cluster of accounting, finance, and management courses; three-course finance, computer science, or management cluster; any major plus two accounting and two finance or economics courses; any major plus accounting and finance, economics, statistics, or marketing courses; masters in accounting, finance, marketing, management or business administration; any major plus three post-baccalaureate courses

Government, policy, and politics	Legislative aide, policy aide, policy analyst, researcher, campaign aide, fundraising, event planning, lobbyist and advocate, budget analyst, intelligence gathering, intelligence analysis, constituency affairs, polling and analysis	Federal agencies; state and local agencies; federal, state, and local office holders; lobbying and advocacy groups; think tanks/research firms	Major or minor in economics, government, political science, history, psychology, philosophy, religious studies, communication, public relations, or business; three-course government, political science, business, or communication cluster; major in psychology, sociology, anthropology, economics, English, government history, or political science and business, communication, economics or finance course; any major plus two to three post-baccalaureate courses
Health care	Physician, physician's assistant, physical therapist, respiratory therapist, nurse, technician and technologist, health educator, social worker, customer service for health insurance provider, supply/equipment sales and training	Insurance companies, hospitals, clinics, government agencies, educational institutions, think tanks	Specialty occupational majors; major or minor in biomedicine, biology, biochemistry, chemistry, or science plus two biology, chemistry, organic chemistry, and physics courses; three-course biochemistry, chemistry, or science cluster; any major plus three to six post-baccalaureate courses in business or economics; mathematics major and two chemistry or biology courses; master's in related areas; certificate in specialized areas
High Technology and Telecommunications	Hardware engineer, software engineer, research and development, promotions and marketing, consulting, Web design and maintenance, support/help specialists	Computer, electronics, and component manufacturers; consulting firms	Major or minor in engineering, computer science, or information technology; three-course engineering, computer science, or information technology cluster; any major plus three to six post-baccalaureate courses

Hospitality and tourism	Hotel management, travel agent, restaurant management, chef, reservations, event planning, sales and marketing, information technology, programming and support	Airlines, hotels, resorts, tourist bureaus, travel agencies, cruise lines, public relations firms, advertising agencies, government agencies, publications	Major or minor in hospitality and tourism, advertising, marketing, business, or communications; three-course hospitality and tourism or marketing cluster; three-course advertising or communication cluster; psychology, sociology, anthropology, or English major plus marketing and management and hospitality and tourism three-course cluster; any major plus three to four post-baccalaureate courses; certificate in hospitality and tourism
Information technology, computers, and consulting	IT consulting, LAN management, systems administrator, systems analyst, sales help and user support, Web designer and administrator	Computer manufacturers and retailers; large corporations; educational institutions; financial service firms and banks; local, state, and national agencies; consulting firms	Major or minor in information technology, engineering, or computer science; three-course information technology, engineering, computer science cluster; any major plus three to six post-baccalaureate courses
Insurance	Sales, underwriter; adjuster; claims; customer service; life, property, automobile insurers; reinsurers; health care and dental insurers	Colleges and universities, consulting firms, financial services companies, goernment agencies, hospitals, insurance agencies, investment banks, large corporations, not-for-profit organizations	Major or minor in insurance, finance, accounting, marketing, business, economics and mathematics; three-course finance cluster; three-course business or management cluster; psychology, sociology, mathematics or English major plus an accounting, marketing, and management cluster; any major plus two to four post-baccalaureate courses

Investment management	Sales, fund manager, analyst, fund accountant	Financial services firms, insurance companies, online brokerage firms, commercial banks, private banks, investment banks, savings and loans	Major or minor in business, economics, mathematics, computer science, or finance; three-course cluster of accounting, finance, and management courses; three-course finance, computer science, or management cluster; any major plus two accounting and two finance or economics courses; any major and accounting, finance, economics, and marketing course; masters in accounting, finance, marketing, management or business administration; any major plus three post-baccalaureate courses
Law, law enforcement, and probation	Lawyer, paralegal, legal assistant, legal researcher, investigator, police officer, probation officer, advocate	State and local agencies, courts, federal agencies and departments, federal courts, law firms, educational institutions	Specialized vocational major or minor; major or minor in political science, sociology, psychology, or anthropology; three-course cluster of sociology/criminology courses; three course cluster of political science, sociology, and psychology courses; any major plus three post-baccalaureate courses; certificate programs
Management consulting	Research analyst, research associate, benefits and compensation analyst, economics and litigation support	Management consulting firms, accounting firms, government agencies, think tanks	Major or minor in business, economics, mathematics, computer science, statistics, or finance; three-course cluster of management or economics courses; any major plus two business, statistics, or economics courses; master's in management or business administration; any major plus three to four post-baccalaureate courses

Manufacturing	Purchasing, contract analyst, quality assurance, engineering, research and development, operations, finance and budgeting, contract development and monitoring	Manufacturing firms, consulting firms	Three-course cluster in engineering or computer science, business management, or economics; any major plus three to six post-baccalaureate courses
Media and Entertainment	Performer, production assistant, writer/editor, reporter, design and production, artist development, artist representation, concert and special-events planning, advertising and promotions, media planning and sales	Radio and television stations, multimedia companies, record and video companies, agents, public relations firms, advertising agencies, publications	Major or minor in media, communication, public relations, advertising, marketing, or business; three-course media, marketing, advertising, public relations, or communication clusters; major in psychology, sociology, anthropology, English, history, or political science plus two media, public relations, communications, advertising, or marketing courses; any major plus two to three post-baccalaureate courses; master's in media, communication, or marketing
Not-for-profit	Program manager, fundraiser, community educator, trainer, grant writer, grant reviewer	Organizations, foundations, government agencies, educational institutions, human service agencies, health-care providers	Major or minor in political science, psychology, philosophy, religious studies, communication, public relations, or business; three-course business, marketing, or communication clusters; major in psychology, sociology, anthropology, English, history, or political science and business, communication, economics, or finance course; any major plus two to three post-baccalaureate courses

Public relations	Event planner, media relations, writer, promotions, design, production	Educational institutions, corporations, media and entertainment entities, national agencies, public relations firms, publishers	Major or minor in communication, public relations, advertising, marketing, business, or economics plus three-course marketing cluster; three-course advertising cluster; three-course public relations or communication clusters; major in psychology, sociology, anthropology, English, history, or political science and a public relations, communications, advertising, and marketing course; any major two to three post-baccalaureate courses; master's in communication or marketing
Publishing	Editor; editorial assistant; researcher; proofreader; public relations and promotions; acquisitions; sales; production; art, design, graphics, and illustration; agent	Book publishers, magazine publishers, Web developers, government agencies, public relations firms, educational institutions	Major or minor in English, communications, public relations, history, business, or economics; three-course business, public relations, or communications clusters; major in psychology, sociology, anthropology, English, history, or political science plus two communications courses; any major plus two to three post-baccalaureate courses; publishing institute or seminar certificate
Real estate	Agent, mortgage broker, appraiser, property manager, development analyst	National, regional, and local agencies; national, regional, and local developers; national, regional, and local property mangers; commercial banks; consumer banks; mortgage banks; financial services firms	Major or minor in real estate, business economics, marketing, or finance; three-course cluster of real estate, finance, and management courses; any major plus two real estate and two finance or business courses; master's in real estate, management, or business administration; any major plus three to four post-baccalaureate courses; certificate

Retail	Sales, buyer, management, promotions and advertising, distribution, finance and auditing, customer service, information technology, operations	Online retailers, department stores, specialty stores	Major or minor in advertising, marketing, business, economics, or communications; three-course marketing cluster; three-course advertising cluster; major in psychology, sociology, anthropology or English plus an advertising and a marketing course
Science and laboratory	Laboratory assistant, research assistant, research and development	Hospitals, universities, pharmaceutical companies, biotechnology firms	Specialty occupational majors with science, biology, chemistry, organic chemistry, and physics courses; major or minor in biomedicine, biology, biochemistry, chemistry or science; three-course biochemistry, chemistry, or science cluster; any major plus three to six post-baccalaureate courses; master's degree in related areas; certificate in specialized areas

As you probably know, IQ usually means "intelligence quotient." Here, however, these letters also stand for "I query." Asking questions and finding the answers (the research part of your ARM strategy) will give you the information you need to choose a major. Review your College Major IQ Test and ask yourself the following questions:

- What five fields are most interesting to me? Why?
- What five entry-level jobs are most intriguing to me? Why?
- What three majors are most closely related to these fields and jobs?
- What academic strategies seem to make the most sense for me to implement now?
- Can I confidently, accurately, and articulately describe my top three majors, career fields, and job functions?
- Have I talked to someone who has majored in one of my top fields or who works in these fields or functions?
- Do I know where I can you get more information about these majors, fields, and functions?

- Are any of my top majors associated with more than two fields of interest?
- What courses would I need to take in order to complete these majors?
- What three-course cluster associated with my top fields could I take?

Go Forward with Confidence

Here are five statements designed to encourage you and send you on your way, confident in the knowledge that you have the skills and focus to find and declare the perfect major for you.

Describe It and Declare It

If you can describe a major, you can declare that major. It's not enough just to say, "I want to major in something that will lead to a good job." Majors are not theoretical constructs. You have to know the prerequisites, required courses, and procedures and policies that are associated with declaring a major or changing majors. Through your research and conversations with knowledgeable people, you'll know enough to be able to describe your desired major clearly. Refer to Chapter 2, and other resources noted throughout this book for help so that you can eventually describe your major and career goals in clear and function-specific ways.

If They Can Do It, You Can Do It

If you have met someone who has majored in a field, you can major in that field, too. Initially your research will be done in books and online, but eventually you need to get some of your information in person. It's important that you meet people who have majored or are majoring in fields that interest you. Talking to them is the best way to find out what those majors are really like and what the coursework entails. Refer to Chapter 3 for some sample questions to get you started. You'll think of plenty of others on your own.

Networking Is a Key to Success

Meeting lots of people exposes you to many viewpoints and opinions. Friends, parents, other family members, alumni, and faculty are usually happy to talk about their academic histories and jobs. The more people you meet who majored in areas of interest to you, the more likely that you will someday follow in their academic footsteps. Talk to several people who majored in one area or who each majored in a different area. Ask them the same questions, and compare their responses. Basically, what you're doing is networking—meeting people who can be helpful to you or exchange information—and this is a skill that you will need throughout your working life. You may even find a role model or mentor in the process.

Research Is Your Most Valuable Tool

Research, performed after assessment, is the central key to your ARM strategy and your ultimate success. Too often students feel pressured by external factors (such as parents, deadlines, or finances) to declare a major, find an internship, or take a job before they are really ready. The only way to get ready is to do your research thoroughly. Take your time, but don't procrastinate. Research, analyze, and prioritize, and then you'll be able to confidently state your academic goals when anyone asks.

There's No Major That Guarantees Future Career Success

There is no doubt that one's choice of a major can influence one's future jobs and career choices, so you should make decisions about your major carefully. Your analysis of the simple tests in this book has revealed interests, values, and skills you may or may not have known you had. As you've seen, any gaps between a chosen major and a desired career can be filled with second majors, minors, clusters, or individual courses. Any skills you may lack for a coveted job can be acquired in any number of ways. The only thing that can come close to guaranteeing your future success is hard work.

Chapter 10

Putting It All Together

It's a truism that one picture is worth a thousand words. Rather than compile your information into a lengthy report, in this chapter you will create a graphic representation of all the data you've accumulated and everything you've discovered about yourself, various majors, and related careers. By the time you finish, you should have a description of the one major that is the best fit for you right now. It's time to put it all together!

The Final Step

Using everything you've done so far, begin to fill in the information requested on the summary worksheets that follow. You may find that you still need to conduct some research in order to fill in all the blanks. While you could guess how your test results link to possible majors, a better idea would be to use your research skills to fill out the forms. If you haven't done it already, explore the careers that relate to your first-glance majors. Next, learn about the required courses needed to complete those majors. In particular, pay attention to whether the information you uncover supports the first impressions that you noted at the beginning of this book and the subsequent test results. Make sure you can answer the following questions:

- Do your first-glance majors match the academic and career subjects that interest you?
- Did the tests reveal other majors that you value, that align with your personality, or that you already have the skills for?
- Can you describe these majors, as well as related careers, in concrete and specific terms that reveal your knowledge of the different fields, functions, and firms?

Can you answer all of the questions related to your major? Complete the worksheets, checklists, and matrix, and you'll find out.

Photocopy each worksheet and checklist before you begin, in case you change your mind and want to complete these activities again.

Summary Worksheets and Checklists

When you began this book, you identified some first-glance majors. Refer back to those pages to complete the exercise below. Enter the top ten majors you identified then. Then score your interest in each of these majors. A score of 10 indicates that you are extremely interested in that major, while a score of 1 means you are not interested at all in that major.

Top Ten First-Glance Majors

Top Ten First-Glance Majors	Score									
	Disinterested			Neutral				Interested		
1.	1	2	3	4	5	6	7	8	9	10
2.	1	2	3	4	5	6	7	8	9	10
3.	1	2	3	4	5	6	7	8	9	10
4.	1	2	3	4	5	6	7	8	9	10
5.	1	2	3	4	5	6	7	8	9	10
6.	1	2	3	4	5	6	7	8	9	10
7.	1	2	3	4	5	6	7	8	9	10
8.	1	2	3	4	5	6	7	8	9	10
9.	1	2	3	4	5	6	7	8	9	10
10.	1	2	3	4	5	6	7	8	9	10
TOTALS	1s	2s	3s	4s	5s	6s	7s	8s	9s	10s

Tally your scores, and pick the five highest scores. If more than five received the highest score, narrow your list down to only five. Next you'll correlate these five majors with your self-knowledge and research into majors and careers.

1.
2.
3.
4.
5.

Top Five First-Glance Majors

Top Five First-Glance Majors	Major-Related Careers From information in Chapter 9, and subsequent use of other resources, identify five career options related to each of your top five first-glance majors.
1.	1. 2. 3. 4. 5.
2.	1. 2. 3. 4. 5.
3.	1. 2. 3. 4. 5.
4.	1. 2. 3. 4. 5.
5.	1. 2. 3. 4. 5.

Top Five Values Statements

Top Five Values Statements Use the top five values identified on your Values Grid (page 93).	Majors and Related Careers From information in Chapter 9, the Values Grid, and other resources, identify majors that match your top values statements and related career options.
1.	1. 2. 3. 4. 5.
2.	1. 2. 3. 4. 5.
3.	1. 2. 3. 4. 5.
4.	1. 2. 3. 4. 5.
5.	1. 2. 3. 4. 5.

Top Five Interest Statements

Top Five Interest Statements Use the top five interests identified on your Interests Grid (page 124).	Majors and Related Careers From information in Chapter 9, the Interests Grid, the Holland code worksheet (page 126), and other resources, identify majors that match your top inter- ests statements and related career options.
1.	1. 2. 3. 4. 5.
2.	1. 2. 3. 4. 5.
3.	1. 2. 3. 4. 5.
4.	1. 2. 3. 4. 5.
5.	1. 2. 3. 4. 5.

Top Five Personality Statements

Top Five Personality Statements Use the top five personality identified on your Interests Grid (page 124).	Majors and Related Careers From information in Chapter 9, the Personality Grid, the Holland code worksheet (page 126), and other resources, identify majors that match your top interests statements and related career options.
1.	1. 2. 3. 4. 5.
2.	1. 2. 3. 4. 5.
3.	1. 2. 3. 4. 5.
4.	1. 2. 3. 4. 5.
5.	1. 2. 3. 4. 5.

Top Five Skills Statements

Top Five Skills Statements Use the top five skills identified on your Skills Grid (page 168).	Majors and Related Careers From information in Chapter 9, the Skills Grid, and other resources, identify the majors that match your top skills and related career options.
1.	1. 2. 3. 4. 5.
2.	1. 2. 3. 4. 5.
3.	1. 2. 3. 4. 5.
4.	1. 2. 3. 4. 5.
5.	1. 2. 3. 4. 5.

Affirmations

Affirmations Review the following major and career statements. In the next column, check those that are true.	✓	Statement Strength Score Identify how strongly you feel about these statements. If you score the statement 5 or less, note what you must accomplish to increase the score to at least an 8. If you need to, turn to Appendix B for a list of resources.		
I can confidently state my top four majors.		Weak Neutral Very Strong 1 2 3 4 5 6 7 8 9 10		
I found and used Web sites and publications related to majors and careers.		Weak Neutral Very Strong 1 2 3 4 5 6 7 8 9 10		
I identified and researched careers related to my top majors.		Weak Neutral Very Strong 1 2 3 4 5 6 7 8 9 10		
I identified the courses required to complete my top majors.		Weak Neutral Very Strong 1 2 3 4 5 6 7 8 9 10		
I am ready to declare a major.		Weak Neutral Very Strong 1 2 3 4 5 6 7 8 9 10		

Compare and contrast your entries in all the summary exercises, and answer the following questions:

Do particular majors appear repeatedly?

What are your top four majors?

What are the courses and careers related to these majors?

Top Four Majors and Careers

Top Four Majors	Major-Related Careers
From all exercises completed, note the four majors you are most interested in.	From information in all exercises, and other major and career resources, identify four related career options for each major.
1.	Related careers: 1. 2. 3. 4.
2.	Related careers: 1. 2. 3. 4.
3.	Related careers: 1. 2. 3. 4.
4.	Related careers: 1. 2. 3. 4.

Top Four Majors and Courses

Top Four Majors	Major-Related Courses
From all exercises completed, note the four majors you are most interested in.	From information in all exercises, and using catalog information from your school or your potential school, list courses required for these majors. Then circle courses already completed.
1.	Required courses:
2.	Required courses:
3.	Required courses:
4.	Required courses:

College Major Matrix

Next you'll create a majors and careers masterpiece, a matrix of all of the most important information that you've gathered up to this point. This will be a representation of all of your assessments that highlights your most compatible majors and careers. Use the information you just added to the worksheets and checklists to fill in the matrix.

College Major Matrix

Top Five Values	Top Four Potential Career Fields	Top Five Interests
1.	1.	1.
2.	2.	2.
3.	3.	3.
4.	4.	4.
5.		5.
Holland Code	**Top Four Potential Job Functions**	**Myers-Briggs Code**
1.	1.	1.
2.	2.	2.
3.	3.	3.
	4.	4.
Top Five Personality Traits	**Top Four Potential Majors**	**Top Five Skills**
1.	1.	1.
2.	2.	2.
3.	3.	3.
4.	4.	4.
5.		5.

Major #1 Course Requirements

With completed courses circled

1.

2.

3.

4.

5.

6.

7.

8.

9.

10.

Major #2 Course Requirements

With completed courses circled

1.

2.

3.

4.

5.

6.

7.

8.

9.

10.

Major #3 Course Requirements

With completed courses circled

1.

2.

3.

4.

5.

6.

7.

8.

9.

10.

Major #4 Course Requirements

With completed courses circled

1.

2.

3.

4.

5.

6.

7.

8.

9.

10.

My First-Choice Major!
The major I will most likely declare:

My Second-Choice Major
Just in case I change my mind, or want a second major, a minor, a certificate, or a cluster:

Look at the matrix. Do you now have all the answers, or do you need to ask a few more questions in order to fill in some spaces? Answer the following questions:

Is your targeted major a realistic and attainable goal?

What additional information do you need?

Are there particular academic obstacles or challenges that might stop you?

What are your next steps?

The next thing you have to do is *take those next steps.* Don't forget that declaring a major is not a lifelong commitment. If you change your mind, you can change your major. Now that you know the ARM strategy of assessment, research, and making decisions, you can revisit the tests in this book again and again if you need to revise and refine your decision.

Above all, congratulate yourself! You have taken positive and decisive steps toward figuring out and declaring your major. Along the way you have probably discovered a great deal about yourself, your interests, and your future. With the information you've gathered and the skills you've learned, you now have *everything* you need to succeed.

Appendix A

Strategic Timelines

No major guarantees a straight path to success, but once you're ARMed with your strategy for assessment, research, and choosing a major, you should be able to progress, anticipate roadblocks, and navigate the crossroads. Wherever you are in your academic journey, here are some points to keep in mind.

High School Students

Think about majors and careers, but don't exaggerate the importance of identifying and declaring a major just yet. Explore your options beyond high school, including colleges, universities, community colleges, and professional training institutions. Add any schools that have majors that interest you, but don't overlook a school just because it doesn't offer a particular major. Look at each schools curriculum to see what prerequisite and required distributive courses it offers. Create your own top twenty list of the courses you might want to take someday, and a top five list of possible majors for each school you think you might apply to. And of course, you can work through the exercises in this book as many times as you need to.

College Freshmen

Take as many diverse courses as you can. If your school has prerequisite or required distributive courses, take any that you find intriguing to see if you might be interested in majoring in the subject area. Read course descriptions, and come up with ideas for courses you will take this semester as well as those you might take in the future.

You don't have to create an ideal schedule for all four years, but you should develop your list of top twenty classes. Don't worry about whether these classes have prerequisites or are available to freshmen. Make a top-five list of majors as well, after completing the exercises in this book. Note any patterns or trends in your lists. Begin to think about "What can I do if I major in _____?" and examine specific courses that would be required of the majors you're thinking about. By the end of your freshman year, you should have a clear top five major list, in addition to a top twenty course list. Don't forget that you can take courses over the summer, too.

Sophomores

Most of you will have to declare a major by the end of this year. Remember that you can change your mind later if you want to. Once you have a particular major in mind, consider if it would be useful to take an additional major, minor, cluster, certificate, or courses over the summer. The first semester of your sophomore year is the ideal time to complete the activities in this book. Create or update your top twenty course list and top five major list before the second semester of sophomore year begins.

The summer between your sophomore and junior years is ideal for internships, shadowing (externships), or talking to people about majors and careers. These practical experiences will have an impact on your ability to prioritize career options and find jobs after college. If you need to, seek the help of career service professionals.

Juniors

Think about whether you want to change majors, add a minor or cluster, or begin a one-course-at-a-time strategy. During this year you should be prepared and able to state your post-baccalaureate graduate school and/or career goals concisely and with confidence. With these goals in mind, you can decide if you have the skills necessary to enter these fields or you need to acquire them. You should be looking for answers to "What can I do with my major?"

The summer between your junior and senior years is a crucial one for exploration and skills-building experiences, or internships. Consult your school's career-services office for internship search strategies, postings, internship-specific resources, and help creating the very best job-search documentation possible, including resumes and cover letters. Explore programs that can bridge the gap from your major to a career, including the University of Dreams (*www.uofdreams.com*), an internship, housing, and educational program with opportunities in New York City, Los Angeles, Chicago, and London (other cities in the United States and overseas may be available in the future), and The Washington Center for Internships (*www. twc.edu*), a program that offers housing, internships, and education programs in diverse fields and settings in Washington, D.C.

Seniors

During the first semester of your senior year you should know "What I can do with my major." You should also know how your minor or selective courses enhance your potential for a successful job search. You need to be thinking about what you'll be doing next year—not necessarily for the rest of your life. If the answer involves graduate study, talk to career services professionals, faculty members, and any specialist advisors about step-by-step efforts, deadlines, and specialized testing. All of this should be done during the first semester. If it involves post-graduation employment only, or in addition to applications to graduate schools, you must do the research to set and articulate your goals early so you can implement effective strategies throughout the year.

Don't forget the value of the one-course-at-a-time strategy. Once you know what you want to do, figure out if a course or two will enhance your potential to get interviews and job offers. Also think about internships during and even after your senior year. A post-baccalaureate internship can be a springboard to a desired job. Network with family, faculty, alumni, and others. Such networking can help you refine your goals, as well as yield advice and even referrals. And don't forget to take advantage of the resources offered by your school's career services office.

Appendix B

Print and Web Resources

Most of the chapters in this book contain brief lists of resources you can use for assessment as well as post-assessment research. Check online bookstores for printed publications and use keywords in online search engines. Your school's career center or library contains a great deal of helpful information, too. Career counselors and reference librarians are professionals trained to help you locate resources. Here is a list of some of the most valuable printed and online resources.

Print Resources

Career Opportunities For . . . Series (Checkmark Books of Facts On File).

Careers For . . . Series (VGM Career Books).

Careers In . . . Series (VGM Career Books).

The College Career Bible (Vault Editors, 2006).

Dictionary of Holland Occupational Codes, Gary D. Gottfredson and John L. Holland (Odessa, FL: Psychological Assessment Resources, Inc., 1989).

Do What You Are, Paul D. Tieger and Barbara Barron-Tieger (Little, Brown and Company, 1995).

Great Jobs . . . Series (VGM Career Books).

Industries and Careers for Undergrads: The WetFeet Insider Guide (WetFeet, Inc., 2005)

Liberal Arts Jobs: What They Are and How to Get Them, Burton Jay Nadler (Peterson's, 1989).

Web Resources

www.career.asu.edu
Arizona State University's "What can I do with this major/degree?" site offers detailed connections between majors and careers.

www.careerservices.rutgers.edu
Rutgers's "Career Opportunities in . . ." series addresses career options for many majors. It also presents profiles summarizing majors and listing related occupations, typical employers, and examples of jobs obtained by graduates.

www.online.onetcenter.org
Users select existing skills and those they plan to develop to identify careers that typically use those skills.

www.careerexplorer.net
Offers a Motivational Appraisal of Personal Potential (MAPP) test that focuses on motivation and corresponding talents.

www.careerkey.org
Contains links and assessments that measure values, interests, personality, and skills.

www.collegeboard.com
The Majors & Careers Central site helps you explore options and identify schools that match your specific needs.

www.discoveryourpersonality.com
The original Myers-Briggs and other career assessments. Provides live follow-up consultations by phone.

www.haleonline.com/psychtest
A free test with results similar to the Myers-Briggs and Kiersey.

www.iseek.org
Includes an exercise that links skills with occupational interests and education-related information.

www.livecareer.com
Identifies career interests and matches them to job functions and careers.

www.nycareeerzone.org
Assists users in identifying interests and reveals how they might relate to the world of work.

www.online.onetcenter.org
Users choose existing skills and those they plan to develop and identify careers that typically use those skills.

www.similarminds.com
Personality test site and community that offers several options.

www.testingroom.com
A site dedicated to self-assessment, with links to numerous online tests and assessments addressing values and personality traits.

www.typefocus.com
Provides a free Myers-Briggs-inspired assessment and other instruments, for a fee.

www.vault.com and *www.wetfeet.com*
Two data-laden sites offering advice on job searching and information on career fields and potential employers.

Index

THE EVERYTHING SERIES!

BUSINESS & PERSONAL FINANCE

Everything® Budgeting Book
Everything® Business Planning Book
Everything® Coaching and Mentoring Book
Everything® Fundraising Book
Everything® Get Out of Debt Book
Everything® Grant Writing Book
Everything® Home-Based Business Book, 2nd Ed.
Everything® Homebuying Book, 2nd Ed.
Everything® Homeselling Book, 2nd Ed.
Everything® Investing Book, 2nd Ed.
Everything® Landlording Book
Everything® Leadership Book
Everything® Managing People Book
Everything® Negotiating Book
Everything® Online Business Book
Everything® Personal Finance Book
Everything® Personal Finance in Your 20s and 30s Book
Everything® Project Management Book
Everything® Real Estate Investing Book
Everything® Robert's Rules Book, $7.95
Everything® Selling Book
Everything® Start Your Own Business Book
Everything® Wills & Estate Planning Book

COMPUTERS

Everything® Online Auctions Book
Everything® Blogging Book

COOKING

Everything® Barbecue Cookbook
Everything® Bartender's Book, $9.95
Everything® Chinese Cookbook
Everything® Cocktail Parties and Drinks Book
Everything® College Cookbook
Everything® Cookbook
Everything® Cooking for Two Cookbook
Everything® Diabetes Cookbook
Everything® Easy Gourmet Cookbook
Everything® Fondue Cookbook
Everything® Gluten-Free Cookbook
Everything® Glycemic Index Cookbook
Everything® Grilling Cookbook

Everything® Healthy Meals in Minutes Cookbook
Everything® Holiday Cookbook
Everything® Indian Cookbook
Everything® Italian Cookbook
Everything® Low-Carb Cookbook
Everything® Low-Fat High-Flavor Cookbook
Everything® Low-Salt Cookbook
Everything® Meals for a Month Cookbook
Everything® Mediterranean Cookbook
Everything® Mexican Cookbook
Everything® One-Pot Cookbook
Everything® Pasta Cookbook
Everything® Quick Meals Cookbook
Everything® Slow Cooker Cookbook
Everything® Slow Cooking for a Crowd Cookbook
Everything® Soup Cookbook
Everything® Tex-Mex Cookbook
Everything® Thai Cookbook
Everything® Vegetarian Cookbook
Everything® Wild Game Cookbook
Everything® Wine Book, 2nd Ed.

CRAFT SERIES

Everything® Crafts—Baby Scrapbooking
Everything® Crafts—Bead Your Own Jewelry
Everything® Crafts—Create Your Own Greeting Cards
Everything® Crafts—Easy Projects
Everything® Crafts—Polymer Clay for Beginners
Everything® Crafts—Rubber Stamping Made Easy
Everything® Crafts—Wedding Decorations and Keepsakes

HEALTH

Everything® Alzheimer's Book
Everything® Diabetes Book
Everything® Health Guide to Adult Bipolar Disorder
Everything® Health Guide to Controlling Anxiety
Everything® Health Guide to Fibromyalgia
Everything® Hypnosis Book

Everything® Low Cholesterol Book
Everything® Massage Book
Everything® Menopause Book
Everything® Nutrition Book
Everything® Reflexology Book
Everything® Stress Management Book

HISTORY

Everything® American Government Book
Everything® American History Book
Everything® Civil War Book
Everything® Irish History & Heritage Book
Everything® Middle East Book

GAMES

Everything® 15-Minute Sudoku Book, $9.95
Everything® 30-Minute Sudoku Book, $9.95
Everything® Blackjack Strategy Book
Everything® Brain Strain Book, $9.95
Everything® Bridge Book
Everything® Card Games Book
Everything® Card Tricks Book, $9.95
Everything® Casino Gambling Book, 2nd Ed.
Everything® Chess Basics Book
Everything® Craps Strategy Book
Everything® Crossword and Puzzle Book
Everything® Crossword Challenge Book
Everything® Cryptograms Book, $9.95
Everything® Easy Crosswords Book
Everything® Easy Kakuro Book, $9.95
Everything® Games Book, 2nd Ed.
Everything® Giant Sudoku Book, $9.95
Everything® Kakuro Challenge Book, $9.95
Everything® Large-Print Crosswords Book
Everything® Lateral Thinking Puzzles Book, $9.95
Everything® Pencil Puzzles Book, $9.95
Everything® Poker Strategy Book
Everything® Pool & Billiards Book
Everything® Test Your IQ Book, $9.95
Everything® Texas Hold 'Em Book, $9.95
Everything® Travel Crosswords Book, $9.95
Everything® Word Games Challenge Book
Everything® Word Search Book

Bolded titles are new additions to the series.
All Everything® books are priced at $12.95 or $14.95, unless otherwise stated. Prices subject to change without notice.

HOBBIES

Everything® Candlemaking Book
Everything® Cartooning Book
Everything® Drawing Book
Everything® Family Tree Book, 2nd Ed.
Everything® Knitting Book
Everything® Knots Book
Everything® Photography Book
Everything® Quilting Book
Everything® Scrapbooking Book
Everything® Sewing Book
Everything® Woodworking Book

HOME IMPROVEMENT

Everything® Feng Shui Book
Everything® Feng Shui Decluttering Book, $9.95
Everything® Fix-It Book
Everything® Home Decorating Book
Everything® Homebuilding Book
Everything® Lawn Care Book
Everything® Organize Your Home Book

KIDS' BOOKS

All titles are $7.95
Everything® Kids' Animal Puzzle &
  Activity Book
Everything® Kids' Baseball Book, 4th Ed.
Everything® Kids' Bible Trivia Book
Everything® Kids' Bugs Book
Everything® Kids' Christmas Puzzle
  & Activity Book
Everything® Kids' Cookbook
Everything® Kids' Crazy Puzzles Book
Everything® Kids' Dinosaurs Book
**Everything® Kids' Gross Hidden Pictures
  Book**
Everything® Kids' Gross Jokes Book
Everything® Kids' Gross Mazes Book
Everything® Kids' Gross Puzzle and
  Activity Book
Everything® Kids' Halloween Puzzle
  & Activity Book
Everything® Kids' Hidden Pictures Book
Everything® Kids' Horses Book
Everything® Kids' Joke Book
Everything® Kids' Knock Knock Book
Everything® Kids' Math Puzzles Book
Everything® Kids' Mazes Book
Everything® Kids' Money Book
Everything® Kids' Nature Book

**Everything® Kids' Pirates Puzzle and
  Activity Book**
Everything® Kids' Puzzle Book
Everything® Kids' Riddles & Brain Teasers Book
Everything® Kids' Science Experiments Book
Everything® Kids' Sharks Book
Everything® Kids' Soccer Book
Everything® Kids' Travel Activity Book

KIDS' STORY BOOKS

Everything® Fairy Tales Book

LANGUAGE

Everything® Conversational Japanese Book
  (with CD), $19.95
Everything® French Grammar Book
Everything® French Phrase Book, $9.95
Everything® French Verb Book, $9.95
**Everything® German Practice Book with
  CD, $19.95**
Everything® Inglés Book
Everything® Learning French Book
Everything® Learning German Book
Everything® Learning Italian Book
Everything® Learning Latin Book
Everything® Learning Spanish Book
Everything® Sign Language Book
Everything® Spanish Grammar Book
Everything® Spanish Phrase Book, $9.95
Everything® Spanish Practice Book
  (with CD), $19.95
Everything® Spanish Verb Book, $9.95

MUSIC

Everything® Drums Book (with CD), $19.95
Everything® Guitar Book
**Everything® Guitar Chords Book with CD,
  $19.95**
Everything® Home Recording Book
Everything® Playing Piano and Keyboards
  Book
Everything® Reading Music Book (with CD),
  $19.95
Everything® Rock & Blues Guitar Book
  (with CD), $19.95
Everything® Songwriting Book

NEW AGE

Everything® Astrology Book, 2nd Ed.
Everything® Dreams Book, 2nd Ed.
Everything® Love Signs Book, $9.95

Everything® Numerology Book
Everything® Paganism Book
Everything® Palmistry Book
Everything® Psychic Book
Everything® Reiki Book
Everything® Tarot Book
Everything® Wicca and Witchcraft Book

PARENTING

Everything® Baby Names Book, 2nd Ed.
Everything® Baby Shower Book
Everything® Baby's First Food Book
Everything® Baby's First Year Book
Everything® Birthing Book
Everything® Breastfeeding Book
Everything® Father-to-Be Book
Everything® Father's First Year Book
Everything® Get Ready for Baby Book
Everything® Get Your Baby to Sleep Book,
  $9.95
Everything® Getting Pregnant Book
Everything® Homeschooling Book
Everything® Mother's First Year Book
Everything® Parent's Guide to Children
  and Divorce
Everything® Parent's Guide to Children
  with ADD/ADHD
Everything® Parent's Guide to Children
  with Asperger's Syndrome
Everything® Parent's Guide to Children
  with Autism
Everything® Parent's Guide to Children with
  Bipolar Disorder
Everything® Parent's Guide to Children
  with Dyslexia
Everything® Parent's Guide to Positive
  Discipline
Everything® Parent's Guide to Raising a
  Successful Child
**Everything® Parent's Guide to Raising
  Boys**
**Everything® Parent's Guide to Raising
  Siblings**
Everything® Parent's Guide to Tantrums
Everything® Parent's Guide to the Overweight
  Child
Everything® Parent's Guide to the Strong-
  Willed Child
Everything® Parenting a Teenager Book
Everything® Potty Training Book, $9.95
Everything® Pregnancy Book, 2nd Ed.

Bolded titles are new additions to the series.
All Everything® books are priced at $12.95 or $14.95, unless otherwise stated. Prices subject to change without notice.

Everything® Pregnancy Fitness Book
Everything® Pregnancy Nutrition Book
Everything® Pregnancy Organizer, $15.00
Everything® Toddler Book
Everything® Toddler Activities Book
Everything® Tween Book
Everything® Twins, Triplets, and More Book

PETS

Everything® Boxer Book
Everything® Cat Book, 2nd Ed.
Everything® Chihuahua Book
Everything® Dachshund Book
Everything® Dog Book
Everything® Dog Health Book
Everything® Dog Training and Tricks Book
Everything® German Shepherd Book
Everything® Golden Retriever Book
Everything® Horse Book
Everything® Horse Care Book
Everything® Horseback Riding Book
Everything® Labrador Retriever Book
Everything® Poodle Book
Everything® Pug Book
Everything® Puppy Book
Everything® Rottweiler Book
Everything® Small Dogs Book
Everything® Tropical Fish Book
Everything® Yorkshire Terrier Book

REFERENCE

Everything® Car Care Book
Everything® Classical Mythology Book
Everything® Computer Book
Everything® Divorce Book
Everything® Einstein Book
Everything® Etiquette Book, 2nd Ed.
Everything® Inventions and Patents Book
Everything® Mafia Book
Everything® Mary Magdalene Book
 Everything® Philosophy Book
Everything® Psychology Book
Everything® Shakespeare Book

RELIGION

Everything® Angels Book
Everything® Bible Book
Everything® Buddhism Book
Everything® Catholicism Book

Everything® Christianity Book
Everything® Freemasons Book
Everything® History of the Bible Book
Everything® Jewish History & Heritage Book
Everything® Judaism Book
Everything® Kabbalah Book
Everything® Koran Book
Everything® Prayer Book
Everything® Saints Book
Everything® Torah Book
Everything® Understanding Islam Book
Everything® World's Religions Book
Everything® Zen Book

SCHOOL & CAREERS

Everything® Alternative Careers Book
Everything® College Major Test Book
Everything® College Survival Book, 2nd Ed.
Everything® Cover Letter Book, 2nd Ed.
Everything® Get-a-Job Book
Everything® Guide to Being a Paralegal
Everything® Guide to Being a Real Estate Agent
Everything® Guide to Starting and Running a Restaurant
Everything® Job Interview Book
Everything® New Nurse Book
Everything® New Teacher Book
Everything® Paying for College Book
Everything® Practice Interview Book
Everything® Resume Book, 2nd Ed.
Everything® Study Book
Everything® Teacher's Organizer, $16.95

SELF-HELP

Everything® Dating Book, 2nd Ed.
Everything® Great Sex Book
Everything® Kama Sutra Book
Everything® Self-Esteem Book

SPORTS & FITNESS

Everything® Fishing Book
Everything® Golf Instruction Book
Everything® Pilates Book
Everything® Running Book
Everything® Total Fitness Book
Everything® Weight Training Book
Everything® Yoga Book

TRAVEL

Everything® Family Guide to Hawaii
Everything® Family Guide to Las Vegas, 2nd Ed.
Everything® Family Guide to New York City, 2nd Ed.
Everything® Family Guide to RV Travel & Campgrounds
Everything® Family Guide to the Walt Disney World Resort®, Universal Studios®, and Greater Orlando, 4th Ed.
Everything® Family Guide to Cruise Vacations
Everything® Family Guide to the Caribbean
Everything® Family Guide to Washington D.C., 2nd Ed.
Everything® Guide to New England
Everything® Travel Guide to the Disneyland Resort®, California Adventure®, Universal Studios®, and the Anaheim Area

WEDDINGS

Everything® Bachelorette Party Book, $9.95
Everything® Bridesmaid Book, $9.95
Everything® Elopement Book, $9.95
Everything® Father of the Bride Book, $9.95
Everything® Groom Book, $9.95
Everything® Mother of the Bride Book, $9.95
Everything® Outdoor Wedding Book
Everything® Wedding Book, 3rd Ed.
Everything® Wedding Checklist, $9.95
Everything® Wedding Etiquette Book, $9.95
Everything® Wedding Organizer, $15.00
Everything® Wedding Shower Book, $9.95
Everything® Wedding Vows Book, $9.95
Everything® Weddings on a Budget Book, $9.95

WRITING

Everything® Creative Writing Book
Everything® Get Published Book, 2nd Ed.
Everything® Grammar and Style Book
Everything® Guide to Writing a Book Proposal
Everything® Guide to Writing a Novel
Everything® Guide to Writing Children's Books
Everything® Guide to Writing Research Papers
Everything® Screenwriting Book
Everything® Writing Poetry Book
Everything® Writing Well Book

Available wherever books are sold!
To order, call 800-289-0963, or visit us at **www.everything.com**
Everything® and everything.com® are registered trademarks of F+W Publications, Inc.